"We can remake our schools [...] affirming, empowering environments in which children can grow and flourish. Please study Dr. Comer's prescription."
—Marian Wright Edelman, President, Children's Defense Fund

"The nation's foremost school reformer goes to the heart of the matter in *Waiting for a Miracle*." —Hugh B. Price, President, National Urban League

"A human and practical approach toward our children. Everyone who cares about America's future should read this book." —Thomas H. Kean, President, Drew University; former governor of New Jersey

"*Waiting for a Miracle* is must reading for anyone who is concerned about the future of American education. . . . Comer is courageous, intelligent, and very experienced. . . . A subject of real importance." —Irving Brooks Harris, Chairman, The Hattis Foundation

"Comer makes an excellent case. He issues a challenge to create a national, comprehensive approach to education that puts the development of the child as the main focus."
—*Emerge*

"This is a book America needs to read. An important work. As I read it, I found myself a regular 'Amen' chorus."
—Linda Darling-Hammond, William F. Russell Professor in the Foundation of Education, Teachers College, Columbia University

JAMES P. COMER, M.D., is the founder of the Yale University Child Study Center, and is now Maurice Falk Professor of Child Psychiatry there, as well as Associate Dean for Student Affairs at the Yale Medical School. A researcher, consultant, and adviser to programs serving children nationwide and internationally, he is the author of *Maggie's American Dream* and co-author of *Raising Black Children*, both available in Plume. Dr. Comer has won numerous awards, most recently the prestigious 1996 Heinz Award for Service to Humanity.

WAITING

FOR A

MIRACLE

WHY
SCHOOLS CAN'T
SOLVE OUR
PROBLEMS—AND
HOW WE CAN

JAMES P. COMER, M.D.

A PLUME BOOK

PLUME
Published by the Penguin Group
Penguin Putnam Inc., 375 Hudson Street, New York, New York 10014, U.S.A.
Penguin Books Ltd, 27 Wrights Lane, London W8 5TZ, England
Penguin Books Australia Ltd, Ringwood, Victoria, Australia
Penguin Books Canada Ltd, 10 Alcorn Avenue, Toronto, Ontario, Canada M4V 3B2
Penguin Books (N.Z.) Ltd, 182–190 Wairau Road, Auckland 10, New Zealand

Penguin Books Ltd, Registered Offices: Harmondsworth, Middlesex, England

Published by Plume, an imprint of Dutton NAL,
a member of Penguin Putnam Inc.
Previously published in a Dutton edition.

First Plume Printing, September, 1998
10 9 8 7 6 5 4 3 2 1

 REGISTERED TRADEMARK—MARCA REGISTRADA

The Library of Congress has catalogued the Dutton edition as follows:

Comer, James P.
    Waiting for a miracle : why schools can't solve our problems—and
how we can / James P. Comer.
        p.   cm.
    Includes bibliographical references and index.
    ISBN 0-525-94144-4 (hc.)
    ISBN 0-452-27646-2 (pbk.)
    1. Child rearing—United States.   2. Child development—United
States.   3. Community and school—United States.   4. Educational
change—United States.   5. Public schools—United States.
I. Title.
HQ769.C6325   1997
306.43—dc21   97–17789
                                                              CIP

Printed in the United States of America

CONTENTS

PART ONE

PERSPECTIVES

CHAPTER

1

MY VIEW

I have been more fortunate than most Americans. My experience as an African-American has been an expression of what America could be. And that is why I want to discuss how it still can become what it set out to be, the Good Society.

I am from a working-class family. On one side I am a generation removed from extreme poverty and abuse, with grandparents probably born into slavery. On the other side I had great-grandparents whose slave experience was less disorganizing, and a grandfather who was a small farmer and church minister.

My choice of child psychiatry as a career stemmed originally from my curiosity about why equally talented (sometimes more talented) black friends did not achieve their potential. In time, my work led to an effort to do something to improve the chances of such young people.

In many ways my life has been a journey from the margins of society toward the center. What I have been told along the way by various people has often been different from what I have observed and what I know will and will not work. So, throughout this book, I will use as a frame of reference my own life experience. This experience in general, and my work in schools in particular, has brought me to doubt that many institutional policies and programs being used and proposed to address our growing social problems—community and family deterioration, educational underachievement, ethnic and racial tensions, vandalism and violence—will succeed.

After several years as director of Yale's School Development Program, I with my colleagues learned how to significantly improve two schools, and then many more. But as we analyzed our work, troublesome questions began to arise. Why did some improve dramatically, some modestly, and some not at all? Why is it so difficult and why does it take so long to improve schools? And most important, why are there so many schools in trouble?

All along we have observed that most schoolteachers and administrators want to succeed. Most parents certainly want their children to succeed. And most students are able and struggling to succeed in all the ways available to young people. What, then, is the problem?

The question calls to mind an apocryphal story.

Two men in a boat rescued a child drowning in a river. As they rowed on, they saw three, then four, and finally a riverful of drowning children. As the man at the oars started for the shore, the other asked him where he was going: there were still so many children to be rescued. The reply was, "I'm going to find out who is throwing these children in the water, and stop them!"

No single person can "stop them"—put an end to institutional and individual problems. But it is important to point out that the state of our schools is not the problem itself, but a reflection of the condition of the larger society. It gradually became clear to me what the problem is.

In our culture we believe that the life outcome of an individual is due almost entirely to genetically determined intelligence and will. This central belief both flows from and contributes to the *individualism* that is so much a part of the American character. (The belief, not coincidentally, is fundamental to our "trickle-down" economic system, according to which, the brightest and the best create and manage economic enterprises and others fit into the system as they are able.) We deny or downplay all other determinants: child development, access to opportunity networks—educational, economic, political, social—and chance, particularly inheritance and the natural connections stemming from where you are born on the social scale.

I call this belief our First Myth.

The many roots of American individualism have been described, often, as both our major strength and our major weakness. The tension that sets individual effort and rights and interests against the common good is probably necessary and even useful—when in balance, and when all individuals have reasonable access to the same opportunities. But a serious imbalance or limited access, for whatever reasons, creates problems.

The notion that intelligence and will alone determine outcomes implies that everyone has similar opportunities and faces similar obstacles. It suggests that the cream rises to the top through superior intellect and exertion, and that is good for society. For their efforts, the best and brightest deserve all they can get. This creates a winner/loser rather than a win-win mentality. The focus on competition allows individualism to run amok—to be carried to extremes that endanger the common good.

Competition is a highly regarded American value. It is a product of the impulse for survival. But the winner/loser mind-set creates a need to find and attack "losers." The loser deserves disdain and exclusion. Gone is any emphasis on caring and on using individual talents to promote the common good. Gone is any recognition that human beings function best in caring societies—in win-win situations.

The universal human task is to find personal adequacy and meaning in life. These are found most often through pride in work, in care for self and/or family, and in being a valued and contributing citizen of a society—a winner. Some people, for a variety of reasons both personal and situational, are unable to achieve this. Yet the myth holds that they have brought all their problems on themselves.

Those who do not succeed at life's tasks often seek adequacy and meaning through behaviors that are troublesome to the society and the individual—that contribute to problems ranging from poor family functioning to undereducation, dependency, crime, and violence. Also, the fear of being a loser can evoke the immature but very powerful human urge to scapegoat others less able to defend themselves.

The effectiveness of this tactic should not be underestimated. Scapegoating is a primitive but natural response to threat and insecurity. A simple example from my own life illustrates this. As a student in graduate school at the University of Michigan with a 3½-year-old son, a newborn daughter, and a wife who had just given birth, I was under stress. One evening I snapped at my son unfairly. He was hurt. Without saying a word, he moved slowly the long way around the room until he reached the crib of his new sister. Then he reached in and hit her.

Because this kind of hurtful reaction is natural, a society must be structured to enable people to deal with insecurity in more mature ways. To minimize scapegoating and to promote the general well-being, a society must make it possible for most people to be successful most of the time. But for many reasons—size, wealth, and particularly the fact that we are a nation of immigrants—America has always resorted to scapegoating. Throughout our history, the latest immigrant group was blamed for any and all problems. The descendants of African slaves have been particularly vulnerable. This caste group would become for the nation what the "problem child" is to a family that is not functioning well—a permanent scapegoat. A common refrain in clinical practice is "There's nothing wrong with us, it's him."

This brings us to what I call the Second Myth—that whites have been successful, and blacks have not.

How is this explained in the face of contradictory evidence? Certainly a large factor has been the First Myth—that able individuals will rise by their own effort. And many whites maintain the myth through their identification with more highly successful whites and through their denial of significant black success.

There have been changes since World War II. A *1996* National Opinion Research Center report indicated that only 7 percent of Americans born after 1945 attribute lower average socioeconomic attainment among blacks to lesser intelligence, compared to 26 percent among those born before. But a sobering 47 percent attributed the disparity to a lack of motivation.

Implicit in this belief is the idea that everyone has had the same chance. This is clearly not true, yet it provides justification for limiting efforts to promote educational and economic opportunities. Racial abuse, even demonization, serves selfish political and economic purposes and encourages continued scapegoating. And blacks are the proxy for all vulnerable groups.

The front cover of the August 12, 1996, issue of *The New Republic* pictured a black woman smoking a cigarette, looking aimlessly into space, with a baby in her lap sucking on a bottle. Blazoned above were the words DAY OF RECKONING, and the story title below read "Sign the Welfare Bill Now." While the articles inside were balanced and thoughtful, the impact of the cover was much more powerful. It is flagrant scapegoating, for it blames people whom many already view as "bad" for the outcomes of past and present bad policies.

Opportunists have managed to convince the average American that "those people" are breaking the bank. In fact, Aid to Families with Dependent Children, Supplemental Security Income, and food stamps—programs for the most dependent—all together amount to 3.4 percent of the federal budget. And most of the recipients are not black, but it is easier to scapegoat them if the public thinks they are. The typical child on AFDC is white and lives in the rural South, Appalachia, or poor areas of major cities. Medicare, Social Security, and other middle-class benefits are actually much more costly than these programs.

The intelligence-determines-outcome myth, with atten-

dant ramifications that are often played out without con-
scious awareness, permeates all our institutions—economic,
political, educational—and affects the way we interact with
each other. It affects our attitudes about health care, child
care, housing, recreation, and all the other things needed to
promote child and youth development and expression and
adequate family functioning.

Alas, it is often expressed most sharply and hurtfully in
schools.

On a recent trip to Copenhagen, I told my hosts—a
teacher and three administrators—about an incident in an
American school: When a teacher brought her dog to school
prior to the opening of the year, a colleague playfully commented, "I see you brought us another student," to which
the dog owner replied, "Oh, no! This is a smart dog, not like
our kids."

The Danish teacher, who had been sitting in a relaxed
position, bolted erect and said sharply, "She should not be a
teacher!" She added that in Denmark some teachers perform poorly but that she had never heard anyone make a
remark like that about students in her many years in the
profession. But when I recount the incident to American
educators, there is little surprise or shock, even if they are
distressed. Most have heard the dummy-loser attitude expressed time and again.

In this case the offending teacher was white and her
school was predominantly black. But in a recent *New York
Times* article about moving her family to the exurbs of up-
state New York, Francine Prose describes how a teacher
there sprinkled a little water on the "slow" students while
watering the classroom plants. She called this practice
"watering the vegetables."

It would be easy to label these teachers "bad." And surely
anything that hurts the development of students is bad
pedagogical practice. But such teachers are products of a
pervasive cultural belief. From their own childhood experiences through their professional preparation to our almost

fanatical preoccupation with the highest test scores in school, they absorb the message that will and intelligence determine success.

In his book *Emotional Intelligence*, Daniel Goleman wrote, "One of psychology's open secrets is the relative inability of grades, IQ, or SAT scores, despite their popular mystique, to predict unerringly who will succeed in life. . . . There are widespread exceptions to the rule that IQ predicts success— many (or more) exceptions than cases that fit the rule. At best, IQ contributes about 20 percent to the factors that determine life success, which leaves 80 percent to other forces." Yale psychologist Robert J. Sternberg and University of Connecticut psychologist Joseph S. Renzulli point to a threshold level of intelligence needed for life success but indicate the importance of factors such as creativity, task commitment, and positive reinforcement as determinants also. I would add good social skills, good health, access to opportunity, and good luck.

As long as most people could work without a high level of education, we got away with the argument that the cream rises to the top. But child care, health care, and community renewal programs are needed to enable most families without education and skills to function well. When our failure to provide such support began to result in social problems ranging from welfare dependency to crime, we blamed and scapegoated the most vulnerable people rather than developing policies and practices needed to adjust to changes created by technological advances.

Now employment requires a higher level of education, so an understanding we have downplayed—that through good development most people can perform well—needs to permeate our institutions. For the common good, society needs to systematically promote adequate development. Blaming vulnerable groups only interferes with our ability to identify and overcome or limit system-level problems that are affecting *all* groups.

For example, the one-parent family incidence among

blacks that Daniel Patrick Moynihan courageously pointed out as a problem about twenty-five years ago is now the rate among whites. The proportion of white one-parent families increased from 10 percent in 1970 to 25 percent in 1994. The *Trends* report issued by the U.S. Department of Health and Human Services indicates that the percentage of births to unmarried white teens rose by 284 percent between 1970 and 1992. In 1970 the rate of black unmarried teen births was three times that of whites. In 1992 it was only one and a third times that of whites.

Substance abuse, once thought prevalent mainly in black communities, is now high in all communities. *Youth Indicators* (1993) noted that in 1992, 88 percent of high school seniors acknowledged using alcohol, 62 percent cigarettes, and 33 percent marijuana. Because blacks make up only 12 percent of the population, these drugs must be in widespread use in the white community.

The arrest rate for violent crimes by white teens under the age of eighteen rose by 300 percent from 1970 to 1992, while the rate for nonwhites rose only 22.5 percent during the same period. And the homicide rate among white males fifteen to nineteen years old almost tripled in those years.

When social problems began to increase sharply in white suburbs and rural areas in the 1970s, it should have been clear that we had underlying structural and/or systemic problems. But it wasn't until the 1990s that policymakers and even social scientists began to give significant attention to these issues. Even now many insist that the problems are individual, unrelated to economic and social structures and processes.

To survive and thrive as a democracy, a society must attend to three areas.

- It must develop *a sound and growing economy* that permits the participation of all of its citizens.
- It must maintain *sound community and family functioning* so that critical tasks, particularly child rearing, can be well performed.

- It must have *a culture that values both* and facilitates the critical interaction between the two.

And do we need to attend to these three areas simultaneously? Yes; they are linked.

- When the economy works, heads of households can earn the resources to promote adequate family functioning.
- When families function well, children are more likely to grow up prepared for success in school, as citizens— and at work.

A serious and sustained imbalance of power and lack of attention to any of these critical areas can lead to big problems. Our society gives lip service to the critical relationship between individual development and opportunity, but does not promote such development widely enough to meet today's requirements. Traditional schooling and the imparting of social skills are both needed, as are the employment opportunities, health care, and child care that help families to make their children ready for school. Unfortunately, we tend to leave these necessities to economic chance.

The fact that individual development is directly related to the quality of community and family functioning is only now being recognized, and even now by too few. Our societal problems, based on wrongheaded cultural beliefs, have indeed been self-inflicted.

Nonetheless, the United States has probably come closer to creating the Good Society than any society of its complexity in the history of the world—despite its huge size, its growing population, and its complicated history of immigration and migration and slavery. Our country is still a place where you can start with nothing and build a fortune. It is still a place where you can worship as you please, speak your mind about what you think is right, even write a book about what you think is wrong.

Even with our great diversity, the United States is still a

place where the democratic ideal remains alive. Indeed, we have endured two centuries of turbulence and struggle—against slavery and for suffrage—times of economic upheavals and divisive wars, and remained strong in our ideals and institutions. America is an idea that has come close enough to its proclaimed promise to tease us into believing that, with just a little more effort, maybe we can get it right. But it is getting late in the day.

The beginning of the twenty-first century is going to be an important psychological watershed. Nations in which large numbers of people are in great trouble are going to go on a downhill course, slowly at first, perhaps, but then rapidly as an increasing percentage of each generation fails to make the grade. Nations that reach the twenty-first century with most of their people functioning well most of the time are going to thrive.

The First and Second Myths identified above stand firmly in our way. They prevent us from overcoming the ill effects of race-based past policies and practices. They prevent us from creating a system of schooling that is based on what we know about how children develop and learn. They prevent us from promoting the kind of community and family functioning that will enable most families to successfully carry out their critical tasks most of the time, now and in a future that will bring great changes and, probably, less work as we now know it.

Without significant change in our culture, neither schools nor any other institutions can solve our problems. Expecting schools to do so is like "waiting for a miracle." But we can change our beliefs and behaviors and begin to effectively address our problems.

We can't begin to make the degree of change that is needed, however, without dismantling our paralyzing myths. The myths affect even our tools of understanding. For example, accepting test scores as reliable measures of student ability, prominent researchers once argued that changing the schools couldn't make a difference. They concluded

that what the students brought with them—their inherent
ability and their early experiences at home—were all that
counted. But subsequent studies have shown beyond any
doubt that schools can and do make a difference. The social
environment of schools can promote student development
and effort and improve academic achievement.

The old research reminds me of the comment of a student who was so fed up with social-science thinking that he
dropped out of graduate school. He asked, "Why is it that
they look at the dying flower and ask what is wrong with it?
Why don't they ask whether it has had enough sunlight and
water, whether the roots have taken and the nutrition is adequate?" Because we believe it is all in the genes, we don't
think enough about how societal factors and forces interact
to make desirable outcomes possible.

The pervasiveness of our major myths has suggested the
organization of this book in three sections: Perspectives,
Winners and Losers, and Win-Win. As my argument goes
against the cultural grain, I devote the first section, Perspectives, to grounding. In the second section I explore the
myths built into our cultural foundation. In the third section
I examine three problem areas we must address, and I propose processes we can put in motion that will allow each
American to help prepare us all to meet the challenges of
this age, and the new age bearing down on us.

In the first section I ask the reader to walk in my shoes, to
see what I have seen, to experience what I have experienced.
I do this by describing aspects of my own growing-up experience. I want you to meet my family and my friends, the
people in my church and neighborhood and school. I want
you to feel the support and opposition I experienced in the
world beyond my family, and the critical role my family
played. I want you to see how my experience was both comparable to and different from that of other young people of
the same ability and economic level.

I want you to walk with me into schools where young

people were not doing well. I want you to hear how lessons learned from my experience brought about improved outcomes where many said it couldn't be done.

Equally, I want you to feel the resistance to efforts to improve the outcomes of many more that was expressed by institutions and individuals from the schoolhouse to the White House of the 1970s.

Because of my experience I know that outcomes are determined by more than intelligence and will. From my perspective, winners and losers are made, not born, and there is no such thing as a self-made man or woman. Yet the critical role of political, economic, and social structures in individual performance is largely ignored. Therefore in the second section of this book I explore our First and Second myths, looking at the way development and performance of the individual is affected by powerful structures and conditions in the networks around them.

I also show how the African-American experience differs from that of other groups in the ways that count the most—cultural discontinuity, inadequate opportunity for family and community development, and exclusion from the economic mainstream over time. The way the black experience is different contributes to the myth of inate inferiority and to greater vulnerability of the group to economic and social problems. I show how rapid changes in the economy over the last fifty years have been particularly harmful, and I discuss how this vulnerability hurts the country as much as the black community.

The problem here is that African-Americans are not a separate country—not even the left arm of a right-handed Uncle Sam. The group is more like 12 percent of the nation's heart muscle. And when that much of our heart muscle is in trouble, we're at serious risk of a national heart attack.

In the third section, I will discuss how we can individually and collectively begin to bring about needed adjustments. First, the nation must find ways to decrease the scapegoating of African-Americans—and all other groups—so that we can focus our attention on the problems and opportunities that face us. Second, we must create a system of schooling that can help us solve societal and cultural problems rather than simply reflect them. Finally, we must find a way to promote a win-win culture—competitive but caring and enabling of all—the Good Society.

Our policies and practices are often labeled conservative or liberal. And we wallow in the debate of public versus private. These dichotomies are not helpful. What we do should flow from empirical evidence of what works, as well as from what is ethical and moral. And successful human systems, because of human nature, require constant efforts to maintain the delicate balance among economic, cultural, and community and family forces. This requires public and private interaction and cooperation—and an effort to promote participation and inclusion for all.

Fortunately, structures and practices that are already in place, or have been beneficially used previously, can be modified or used as models to address today's needs. We already spend a great deal of money on social programs; unfortunately, too little is spent to prevent problems in the first place. Our task is to change the cultural mind-set in all our institutions from "those who can, will" to "all can."

Although the school is a reflection of the problem, with adjustments it can become a significant part of the solution. There are studies that show that scientifically based structural changes—organized and managed, and working differently at every level—and not education gimmicks can make public schools effective. And this in turn can foster the broader national change that we need as we face the challenges of the twenty-first century.

A colleague has pointed out that if deep-seated beliefs and related dynamics are the problem, and cultural change is the key to solving it, we are in a tight spot. Culture change is difficult and slow. There can be no "magic bullet," no quick fix.

Yet I am optimistic. With effective mobilization, significant cultural change has already taken place in our country in a reasonable period of time. And as I will show, mechanisms *can* be put in place to begin to solve our problems, to create a good and caring society capable of adjusting in a future that will be changing ever faster.

CHAPTER
2

MY WINDOW

All through my young years the most troublesome problems appeared to stem from my race. I remember thinking that if I were white I would not have them. When I was in kindergarten my mother arranged a classroom birthday party for me. Afterward, a white classmate begged me to walk past his house, and I later realized it was to back up his story. From the upstairs porch, his mother asked me whether I had had a party, and then expressed surprised, saying, "I didn't know colored people did anything but fight and drink all the time." I remember clinging to the fence feeling very small and very sad.

Mom tried to protect us from such experiences. She generally called when we were invited to the birthday parties of white classmates to make certain that their parents knew we were black, and would welcome us. One well-meaning parent greeted all of us at her son's party, and then looked at me and said, "And you are very welcome also." My classmates looked puzzled, unable to understand why I got special attention. But I did. Race was a big burden on my little shoulders.

Eventually I came to understand that race is not the underlying problem. *Race is often used for the economic, social, and psychological advantage of whites in the struggle for power and security,* distracting us from our just benefits. And in a capitalist society nothing is more important than economic power.

I used the distraction tactic myself while working on a fruit truck when I was ten years old. When the truck left the stop in my neighborhood, my friends would run after it to grab fruit off the back. To keep my job and avoid my friends' wrath I had to find a clever way to keep them away from the fruit. As the truck pulled slowly away from the stop, I would throw one peach in their direction and all six or seven would dive after it. By the time they got up, the truck was gone.

This is how opportunists use the issue of race. The difference is that the fruit didn't belong to my friends, but race as a distraction denies blacks and whites conditions that are our birthrights. I had to understand the tactic in order not to be diminished and paralyzed by it.

My search for deeper understanding was sparked in 1960 by a troubling incident during the first week of my internship at St. Catherine's Hospital in my hometown of East Chicago, Indiana. In the emergency room I treated an African-American woman who had been kicked in the abdomen by her husband. I called her physician, a white man who had the largest black practice in town. He didn't know me, didn't know that I was black. He approved my treatment, then instructed me to give her a shot of penicillin. When I demurred because penicillin was not indicated, he added, "*They* all have a little PID"—pelvic inflammatory disease due to venereal disease.

I was stunned. First, he was prescribing on the basis of a stereotype rather than symptoms—which amounted to malpractice. Second, this was a man who held the trust of many blacks. Given his reputation in the black community, I doubted that he was deeply prejudiced. So what caused his hurtful and probably unintended expression of racism?

I was twenty-five years old at the time and better educated than most people, but I could not begin to answer my question. I had never had a course that discussed the black experience and had not gotten around to reading about it. That afternoon I went to the library. Wanting to start from the beginning, I checked out *Black Cargoes*, an examination of the slave trade by Daniel P. Mannix and Malcolm Cowley. I read late into the night, and then tossed and turned in my sleep. I woke up the next morning needing to know more—about Africa, slavery, Reconstruction, Jim Crow laws, violence against blacks, the fight for justice and opportunity, American economic history, particularly as it applied to blacks, and black communities, families, and children.

Another experience toward the end of my internship brought the questions about community, families, and children to the surface. Because I was planning to become a general practitioner in my hometown, and because I needed the money, I did some moonlighting with a black doctor who had the other large black practice in town. One night I made a house call to a low-income part of town. All the lights in the apartment were out. I knocked on the door, and a weak, distant voice asked me to come in. I felt for, found, and turned on the light. Roaches, hundreds of them, covered the walls and made a sickening, screeching sound as they scrambled out of sight. Two small children were sleeping in orange crates by the front door, covered by roaches the moment before. Their mother, the patient, was in the bedroom.

She was depressed—no other problem. I remembered her as a classmate of my brother's in high school, intelligent but not very interested in school. She had gone on a downhill course that many friends from high school had taken, or were about to take: depression, alcohol abuse, unwanted pregnancies, and crime. Three intelligent friends I had known since kindergarten twenty years before now had at least ten children among them. (In time they would have more than twenty. Eventually one friend died from alcoholism, one spent a good part of his life in jail for murder, and the third was in and out of mental hospitals until his recent death.)

What was going on? It could not have been a lack of opportunity. Most were from two-parent families. Their fathers, like mine, worked in the steel mill. True, there were troublesome racial attitudes everywhere you looked for them. But there was also a reasonable abundance of opportunity and fair play. I didn't have a black teacher until I went to Howard University College of Medicine, yet in hundreds of dealings with teachers, I didn't have more than a smattering of school and college experiences that were overtly racist. I probably had an equal number of white teachers who went out of their way to be supportive because they disapproved of racism.

Indeed, I was having the same kind of experiences as an intern. Once while I was making rounds with two white trainees and Dr. Steen, the head of the training program, one of his private patients pointed in our direction and objected to our seeing her. Dr. Steen exploded at what we all thought was a racist act until we realized the woman was objecting to a white intern who looked like he was twelve years old.

Another evening an intoxicated white man in admissions called me a nigger, and a white intern grabbed him and held him for me to punch. Not yet trained to handle such matters, I did. I regretted it, especially the next day when the patient learned of his behavior and apologized profusely.

Toward the end of my internship a highly regarded senior practitioner asked me if I would be interested in joining a medical group that he and several physicians, all white, were forming in a suburban community. I was honored because of the caliber of the people involved, and somewhat surprised because there were no blacks in the communities the group would serve.

So, did I experience racism? Yes, it was everywhere, but not at a high level among everybody.

By that time my concern about the plight of friends and the black poor in general had grown to the point that I abandoned my plan to go into practice and do my military service in the army reserves at home. My new plan was to do my service time in the U.S. Public Health Service and meanwhile figure out how best I could help.

Another five years would pass before I fully realized how much the remarkable child-rearing job my parents had done accounted for my success in the world. Finally I began to understand why so many able African-American young people underachieved, and some of the ways to attack the problem.

I am from a working-class background. My father, Hugh, was a steel mill laborer and janitor. My mother, Maggie, did domestic work before and during the first twelve years of their marriage, until my birth. Dad was from rural Alabama and had about a sixth-grade education, and Mom went to school in rural Mississippi for only a few days during a two-year period. A neighbor of one of her employers helped her become barely literate, and later my older sister Louise, a teacher, taught her to read and write at a marginal level. My father was the son of a minister and from a stable family. My mother's father was a good man, a sharecropper, more educated than most blacks at the turn of the century. But he was killed by lightning in 1910 when my mother was six years old. Because the five children were too young to work the farm, a stepfather who was cruel and abusive in every way came into their lives. They moved from place to place in Mississippi and then to Memphis, Tennessee, under harrowing conditions of poverty.

When my mother was eight years old, she decided that the way to a better life was through education, and at age sixteen she ran away to East Chicago to her older half-sister in the hope of going to school. Though she had to leave school and become a domestic worker, she declared that if she ever had children, she was going to make certain that they all received an education. She then carefully sought a husband of like mind. Because Dad was a divorced man, twelve years older, and with a daughter, Mom insisted that he present letters of recommendation from his mother and his former mother-in-law before they could date. They were married two years later, and eventually reared and supported their children in a way that enabled the five of us to earn thirteen college degrees among us—two schoolteachers, a retired school superintendent, an optometrist-businessman, and myself.

Reflecting on life with Maggie and Hugh made me aware of how very crucial good child rearing and development are. Schools and modern society underestimate these factors. The failure of our leaders to adequately protect and promote supportive families contributes heavily to the problems that now tear at the fabric of our society.

First, and very important, both of my parents wanted children and dedicated their lives to giving us what we needed to succeed. They found personal meaning and purpose in doing so, and this gave us a profound sense of belonging and worth. Also, they had high aspirations for us. I was given the middle name Pierpont, after Pierpont Morgan, considered the richest man in the world when I was born in 1934. Wealth was not all-important to my parents; this name was simply their statement that they wanted their child to *achieve.*

My parents believed in their right to opportunity and to belonging in America as African-Americans. My father said to us on many occasions, "Prepare yourself. Your time will come." He explained that because the nation was built on Judeo-Christian principles, in time it would have to change and provide opportunities for blacks. While this belief didn't always appear realistic, we accepted his admonition with the blind faith young people often accord parental advice. And there was just enough evidence that he might be correct, in school in particular, to keep us hopeful and motivated.

In interviewing my mother for my book *Maggie's American Dream,* I came to appreciate how deliberate their child training was, although at the time it just seemed like growing up to me. My mother believed that the proper balance between order and freedom, pleasure and punishment led to self-discipline, thinking, and development of social skills.

Some people accused me of treating you all like little soldiers—too strict, keeping everything too perfect. Thelma's room couldn't be messed up 'cause hers was off the living room. But you boys could mess up your room because it was toward the back. . . . You had all kinds of fun in there, but not in the living room, dining room, or kitchen, except on special occasions and then you would have to clean up after. There is a time and a place to be clean and work hard, and a time to let down and relax.

Because of the fun times we had with you, it made it easier when we had to chastise you. You knew the chastising was for your sake. In that way we never had a lot of trouble with you fellows like a lot of parents have, especially today. You did very well in school without our having to keep at you. But I spent a lot of time with you from the time you were very young, and kept an interest in your work all the way through.

Your dad was the same way.

They gave us everything they could afford and a lot of things money can't buy. I remember, with great fondness, popcorn and malted milk candies on the porch, trips to the Lake Front park with Mom and Dad, Mom reading the funny papers to us on Sunday evening even though she herself could barely read. It didn't matter because we had her, and we were warm and secure.

They took us to see President Roosevelt's motorcade as it came through town, the natural history museum and the aquarium, the Bud Billiken Day Parade, the Brookfield Zoo, and on and on. They sometimes found a way to provide us with experiences they couldn't afford. I overheard my mother on the telephone lobbying a distant cousin who belonged to the organization that selected a yearly participant in the

Indiana Boys State program. Oddly enough, I was selected
for the honor as a freshman instead of in my junior year, as
was usually the case.

Because we were well brought up, adults liked us, and
black and white friends of the family took us to Cubs games
at Wrigley Field, circuses, the high school basketball playoffs
in downstate Indiana, a Jewish community basketball league
in Chicago.

Dinner was the time we were all together. On birthdays
and like occasions Mom prepared the favorite dish of each
child and managed to make us all feel special. At the dinner
table we were expected to talk about school or anything
else—ideas, concerns, problems—and we didn't have to be
encouraged. The rules of conversation were learned and
practiced: wait, listen, express yourself clearly. The conversations often carried over into after-dinner debates in which
you had to think fast or your sibling would win. You would
ponder about how to make your case better next time,
because losing was not fun in our house, and the rule was
that you could not fight no matter how badly you lost or how
angry you got.

Neither Mom nor Dad ever denied the existence of the
race problem, but we were not to be victimized by it. My
father often said, "Never let your race stop you from doing
anything you want to do." He sometimes said, pointing to his
head, "Get it up here. They can't take that away from you."
When a black person achieved something desirable, Dad
would say, "Just give my people a chance!" And when he
heard about or saw undesirable behavior, he would say sadly,
"My people, my people."

All of these experiences, particularly the informally
supervised debates, provided us with the stuff that academic
success is made of: confidence, interaction skills, thinking
and articulation, attacking and defending arguments, ana-
lyzing and solving problems, cultural literacy, and more.

Equally important, the stuff of character building was in
our everyday family environment. My father often said,

"Nothing beats a failure but a try," and, "The measure of a man is from here [his finger pointing to his neck] up," meaning his intelligence and integrity. If we procrastinated over assignments, Mom would say:

> "Whenever a task is set for you,
> Don't idly sit and view it,
> Or be content to wish it done,
> Just go to work and DO IT."

Every day at the same time Dad would come around the corner of the Gargas Coal Yard at the end of our street on his way home from work; so reliable was he that my mother called the steel mill in alarm on the first occasion that he worked overtime. When he was the Sunday school superintendent he began each session at the exact scheduled hour, and out of respect for him, some people ran to get there on time. My sister Thelma, competing in the Baptist Young People's Bible Drill at our church, recalls that somebody not competing whispered the correct Bible verse at the same time she gave it. Dad, as the moderator, disallowed her answer to avoid an appearance of unfairness. As a child she thought her own father might have given her a break, but she learned that fair is fair, always.

This extended to everyone. Most of our ministers were good and respected people, but one we had was a rogue. He pocketed church money and had an affair with one of the sisters, among other things. The deacon and trustee boards appealed to him privately, but he was popular with the congregation and could afford to ignore them. Finally Dad, a deacon, stood up during the collection, informed the congregation, and called for his ouster. During the uproar that followed, one of my classmates said to me, "Why doesn't your ol' father shut up?" A church sister nearby overheard, turned to her, and said, "*You* shut up! Brother Comer is standing up for right. You must always stand up for right, no matter what." My great embarrassment turned to a pride that stirred my twelve-year-old soul, and the message gained a deep and lasting place inside. The rogue minister, by the way, was dismissed.

Mom had a strong dislike of religious hypocrites, but Dad was more forgiving. He was also generous to a fault, and Mom was always concerned about having enough money to attain long-range family goals. Mom was a fusser, and they disagreed on these and other matters. Dad would smile wryly and reject a point with a simple "ahhh!" Only once, when Dad was very ill and wouldn't slow down, and Mom was desperately worried about the family's future, did a disagreement escalate into a shove and a shove-back. Even when we raised questions about some of Dad's religious beliefs, which Mom thought disrespectful, he encouraged us to speak. Thus, disagreement without disagreeable behavior was the norm at our house.

We were a bit better off than many, because Mom and Dad built our first home themselves, rented out a couple of apartments they owned, and had a little convenience store for a time. Dad worked a few days every week even during the Depression. Dad and Mom helped other family and friends often—if not with money, with housing, food, and caring. My father once wrote, "The measure of a man is his concern for his fellow man." And one of Mom's favorite stories was about a status-conscious lady who was told that God was going to come to her house for dinner. She prepared an elaborate meal. Three people in need came by and asked to be fed, and she sent them away. Finally, when God didn't appear, she called out to ask his whereabouts and a voice came back, "Three times I visited your house today, and three times you sent me away."

Teachers experienced the product of all of this when the Comer kids went to school. Mom told us, "Now, you mind the teacher and pay attention to the lesson. If you don't think the teacher is treating you right, you tell me and I'll talk to the teacher. Not you. Hear me?" We said, "Yes, ma'am." But because we were prepared for school, and

Mom, with Dad's full support, was there for every parent activity, and both were interested in our progress, there were few problems with teachers. And when there was a problem, Mom's way of engaging them—a spirit of problem solving, without acquiescence—made things better for us after the discussion rather than worse.

I have often heard middle-class people characterize such a family life as cultural imperialism, the imposition of middle-class values on low-income people. Of late it has been dubbed "white behavior" by both blacks and whites. I prefer to think of it as preparing low-income people to hold a job and function comfortably in the mainstream, in our shared world.

Certainly my mother's practices were influenced by her experiences working for successful white families. She didn't adopt everything; some practices she considered too permissive. But others were simply the kind that helped a person to function at work and as a citizen—more social skills than middle-class habits. Many European immigrants have gained mainstream cultural skills and behavior through similar associations.

Also, mainstream American culture and our church-based black culture, while sometimes different in style, did not differ in substance in any basic way. Given the religious underpinning of the American Constitution and culture, this is not surprising. Hard work, fair play, individual rights and responsibilities, compassion, delay of gratification to achieve a long-range goal and reward, respectful and respectable living—all these elements of the Judeo-Christian ethic are essential to both cultures.

Growing up with my feet planted in two cultures was beneficial. So was living in a racially integrated neighborhood and going to a racially integrated school. White drunks stumbled from the Lakota Hotel, a flophouse around the corner from our quiet little neighborhood of mostly blacks; occasionally one would want to play with us, but my father would not let them get too close. A white schoolmate lived in a dysfunctional family in a shack on the alley behind our house. We went to birthday parties and belonged to clubs with middle-class white kids. My brothers and I played basketball in the private gymnasium of one of the rich families my mother once worked for. We went tobogganing at the second home of the family of a strong student-government ally. As a result, my perception of white people was not skewed by stereo-types. I had no illusions of greater or lesser ability, greater or lesser morality. I realized that most had a leg up but that I could compete.

Years later when I discussed on a television program how the good-white and bad-black stereotypes were harmful to black youth performance, the black cameraman from Newark almost couldn't wait to tell me his story. When he was at a pre-dominantly white college in Connecticut, he had called his mother after an exam and said, "Guess what, Mom. They cheat!" Imagine—such behavior from perfect whites!

In our family, protection from the damage of stereotypes owed nothing to chance. It was both forcefully taught and indirectly achieved through Mom's school involvement, our own performance, and the raised expectations schoolteachers had for us.

In the fifth grade, a new classmate told me that her mother knew my mother. When I asked Mom, she explained that she had worked for the family years before. She added, "Don't you worry about that. You are just as clean, just as smart, and you can do just as well. And you had better!"

Our experiences in elementary and high school re-inforced the message of our home: You can achieve at a high level. I remember that a science teacher showed a film about the life of George Washington Carver, the renowned black botanist, although it had no relevance to our present work. I was the only black student in that class, and science was my strong area. I knew that she was saying to me, "Yes, you can." Most teachers were fair to me, my siblings, and many other black students. And they were not alone. My mostly white classmates elected me to the student council for six straight years, in spite of the controversies I got into and sometimes led: a drive to have black cheerleaders, an end to segregated swimming (blacks on Friday!), an end to the segregation of the choral club, and more.

The problem of racism remained, however. Things hadn't changed that much since my sister Louise had been denied membership in the National Honor Society seventeen years before because she refused to play the piano for that same segregated choral group. And school officials still covered over the swimming pool during the summer and used it as another basketball court rather than integrate the swimming program.

In addition, not all teachers were so understanding. When I was in an elementary school class with the three friends who eventually went on downhill life courses, we had a library-book-reading contest. I read the most books. My three friends didn't read any. Our teacher was so frustrated that she said, "If you three little colored boys don't want to be like the rest of us, you should not come to our school!" Yet she was not a die-hard racist. Until that point I had walked hand-in-hand to school with her. And if she had understood that these were the children of former share-croppers who were intimidated by great big white institutions like libraries, she would have taken them to the library herself, helped them get their first cards, even helped choose their first books.

My friends were not bad or lazy or obstinate, they were just not *prepared* to connect with the people and work of the school. The teacher saw performance as a simple matter of ability and will, or a lack of both. She had not been *prepared* to understand that her own behavior could affect performance. But she unintentionally sent her pupils a message of rejection, making it likely that they would perform less well in the future.

During my fifth-grade year in 1944, students from the predominantly black and overcrowded Columbus School were sent without any preparation to our predominantly white Washington School—a harbinger of the way national school integration policy would be mismanaged. In our case, I served as a connecting link.

In one class, as exercises in government, we students elected officers each week and gave reports on current events. Except for me, the black students were being called on last or left out altogether. When the pattern was clear, but with some concern about how the teacher and my white friends would react, I stood up and objected to the practice. The teacher, Miss Johnston, was sitting in the back knitting. When I sat down, I looked around to get her reaction. She gave me a wink of approval, and the exclusion practice, only partly explained by the fact that the kids were new to the school, changed.

On another occasion, we were rehearsing a skit and one of the black students, mildly irritated by something, said to another, "Get your hands off me, nigger." The throw-away line brought total silence to the room. Finally I asked that we agree not to use the N-word, and with relief everybody agreed and went back to work.

One new black classmate, Mickey, was bigger and older and tougher than the rest of us. He demanded "protection" gifts from a student named Kyle whose grandfather owned a store downtown. After complying for a while, Kyle told me that he was afraid he was going to get caught stealing from his grandfather and asked for my help. Mickey liked me, but this was a delicate matter. When I got a chance, I told him, "Kyle's all right, and besides, if he gets caught taking something from the store and fingers you, you've got trouble." Mickey's expression suggested that he hadn't thought of that, and he soon gave up the shakedown.

Moving to a mostly white school also had a telling effect on the new students' confidence. My sister Louise had been a teacher of many of them when they were at Columbus School. She would ask me about certain ones she knew had been good students, and was surprised that they were not excelling. I myself had a similar experience in reverse. During the next summer I was in a Sunday-school convention Bible class with five of my classmates from regular school. The Bible class was at their former school, Columbus. The students and the teacher and I all expected me to do best on the examination, because I was one of the best students in regular school. But I came in sixth out of six, last in the class. At the time I was embarrassed but felt that I had simply underestimated the competition. On reflection years later, after my studies in psychology, I realized that they were in "their space"—comfortable and valued, able to connect, confident, and thereby motivated to perform at a high level.

Years later a leading advocate of school integration, a white Southerner, was disappointed when I challenged an argument of his: "If national policy would just put the kids together, racial enmity would go away." By then I had come to understand the race relations of my childhood as extremely complex. Indeed, I eventually realized that school segregation was not the critical problem; it was exclusion of blacks from the economic mainstream. While school integration was important to break the powerful image of white superiority and black inferiority, economic integration was needed to make school integration work, and to improve race relations in general.

Today in many poorly functioning, low-income communities, there is strong pressure not to take school seriously. This was not the case for me, my brothers and sisters, and others. Our black friends were delighted that we were among the top students in our predominantly white school. I remember the banter among our respective peers: "My Comer got more A's than your Comer."

Although the times in some ways permitted more individuality, we were not scorned because we treated other people well and expected to be treated well. It could have been no other way at the home of Maggie and Hugh. We very much enjoyed and were involved in sports. My brother Norman was a three-sports star and good enough to play football for Northwestern University. While we didn't have school dances because of the possibility of interracial dancing, we danced. In fact, I danced so well that in college the spotlight was often put on me, even at the black dances. But we gave greater time and attention to academic learning. Even as a high school junior, I read the lines from Gray's "Elegy in a Country Churchyard"—"Full many a flower is born to blush unseen, / And waste its sweetness on the desert air"—as a metaphor for the underappreciation of people like my parents.

While we were "regular guys," our friends accepted that we lived differently. Until we went off to college, we had a curfew. By then we knew there was a reasonable time to come home. When someone ridiculed us, another would usually say, "Hey, that's the Comers. That's the way they live," meaning, that's okay for them. I also think it meant, maybe it's a good thing that somebody cares. When our friends wanted to play ball, they called us; when they went off for mischief, they didn't. When the Calumet gang came to our Carey Street neighborhood to fight, they stopped to talk to my brother but didn't bother him because we were not a part of that kind of action.

Much of this was due to the powerful presence and expectations of our parents. It exemplified the way a constructive family code protects young people from their own impulses and the bad influences of others; it can even positively influence others. At a reception held for me years later on the East Coast, a professional man who grew up near us in a troubled family stopped the party to tell how our parents and family life had served as the model that helped to make his successful education, career, and family life possible. When my brother recently attended the funeral of a cousin, he learned of the numerous second and third cousins who are getting college degrees in various demanding disciplines. And their parents told him that they were inspired by Aunt Maggie and Uncle Hugh.

Solid families and related institutions hold neighborhoods together and enable them to be constructive, supportive cultures. There is a widespread belief that such black families are rare. But in fact, solid black families were and are the majority. When I began to tell stories from my interviews with my mother during my lectures, African-Americans in the audience and some whites would tell me that their family story was similar to mine. My family and its primary network, the church culture, made achievement possible in the absence of full opportunity in the larger society. Since the 1950s, massive changes in the nature of the economy have limited the ability of families to protect and promote their members, but many poor families are still doing so.

By the time I reached high school, there were a large number of high-achieving black students there, more often from well-functioning families. Some of us joined the East Chicago Tennis Club, founded by the late Bill Passmore, a charismatic paraplegic who inspired us all. Tennis was secondary, self-affirmation primary—especially important in a world that says you and your kind can't achieve.

That message was often more blatant outside of school. One evening during the summer before I went to college a group of us were singing songs around a fire and several white men who had been drinking beer nearby yelled, "Why don't you niggers go back to Gary where you belong?" Many in our group were dean's list students at Indiana University; two went on to make Phi Beta Kappa. Most are now teachers, physicians, lawyers, and business people. Fortunately, three or four of the men in our group were also varsity football players. They didn't say or do anything to our tormentors; they just stood and observed them. The men hurriedly bundled their belongings and went back somewhere themselves.

The way we handled this incident illustrates how black families can be effective in preparing and protecting their children against slurs thrown out in the larger society: "Don't take abuse. But don't handle it in a way to bring more [the police]. Words can't hurt you. You know who you are."

The incident reflected the one area where my parents

were probably too optimistic. "Prepare yourself and you'll be accepted," my dad said. Much earlier on, though, I had an experience that helped me begin to understand that stereotyping blacks and denying them opportunities were tactics to preserve an advantage. When I was eleven years old I overheard my uncle Morgan, visiting from Alabama, tell my father about a neighboring white farmer who frequently expressed concern about the poor living conditions of blacks and stated that if only they lived better, they would be accepted. But when my uncle built a modern ranch-type home, the farmer said, "Morgan, did you have to build the nicest home in the county?"

By the time I was ready for college, my father was suffering from an industrial illness and living in Arizona for a good part of the year. I worked as a stock boy, but for college we needed the sort of wages the steel mill paid. Mom convinced the personnel officer at the mill where Dad had worked for thirty years to give me a summer job although I was just seventeen instead of the required eighteen. I was placed on the laborers' gang rather than in one of the office jobs the white students had. A couple of my classmates were embarrassed by the fact that the system was not based on merit. I was the good student, and they had the good jobs.

A friend of mine finished Purdue University with a degree in chemistry in the 1940s. When he applied for a position as a chemist at the steel mill, the personnel officer was so amused that a black person thought he could become a chemist that he and a coworker shared a hearty laugh. My friend would go back to school and become a dentist.

When I was an intern and applied for a car loan at a hometown bank, the young loan officer expressed pride in my achievement and was confident that my application would be approved. But when he saw me returning, he reached for his milk on ice, then the treatment for gastric ulcers. My loan had not been approved, while a white intern from out of town with the same financial situation received his loan.

High school success left me unprepared for college life in southern Indiana in 1952. Without my being aware of it, much of my positive sense of self was based on being a popular, well-rounded, good student. But at Indiana University there were many such students. Also, racial strain was more obvious: students who preferred to stand in the rain rather than get in a car with me, several restaurants just off campus that would not serve blacks, a dormitory housing policy that would not let blacks and whites live together even when they wanted to. In fact, the dorms had been open to blacks only for a few years. Signs of affluence, power, and privilege were everywhere, symbolized by the mansions of fraternity row, all closed to blacks. I had not come to grips with what it meant to be a black from a working-class family.

Lonely, scared, and depressed, I made all C's the first semester, hardly good enough to get into medical school. I had to do better. During the second semester I took a course from a Professor Bobron, who affected a British accent although he was American. To impress us with his sophistication, he spoke often of "the Continent" and of Josephine Baker, and he criticized American anti-intellectualism, especially the popularity of college athletics. One practice of his was to grade our themes anonymously and read the best one to the class. One time he picked mine, "My Dormitory Buddy." He read it aloud, praising and explaining why it was deserving. About halfway through, however, he had a question and asked for the author. I raised my hand, the only black student in the class. From that point on, despite a big red A on the front, he criticized every remaining line. Instead of a confidence-building victory, my good work brought me a devastating defeat.

Battered by loss of self-esteem, I went home that summer to regroup. Without understanding what I was after, I visited all the sisters and brothers from our church who had praised and helped to raise me. I went to many of the favorite places my parents had taken us as young children, tapping the good feelings from the past. The fact that my family expected me to succeed was reaffirmed. By the end of sophomore year I was on the honor roll.

I was one of the lucky ones. Too many black students played cards when they should have been studying, eventually didn't go to class, and flunked or dropped out after a semester or two. They had wanted to succeed. They were intelligent enough to succeed. They were not lazy. I couldn't understand what was going on. Only later, while studying psychology, did I come to understand. It was avoidance behavior—avoidance of all the negative messages and rejections from the Bobrons of the world. At a lecture, I heard the Harvard psychiatrist Chester Pierce refer to them as mini-aggressions. Card playing was a focused interaction that provided feelings of achievement and social comfort. But as students failed in the academic area, their related sense of power and belonging—already weakened by the miniaggressions—was further weakened.

Fortunately, I was spared the same fate because my parents expected me to find a way to succeed, and I had had enough success in a racially integrated environment to know that I ought to be able to succeed. And I had the help of my church culture, my social network at home. I was protected against the message of the larger world: "You can't, you won't, and who do you think you are anyway?" By that time I had the pride and skill needed to hold on and fight back.

Because of my anger, a number of years passed before I remembered that there were concerned and fair people at the university who helped me to recover and succeed. Once, I was taking one of those pre-med courses we called "major changers"—difficult, and if you didn't do well, you changed your major. On the first examination I made the lowest score in the room. The laboratory instructor, a white graduate student who had talked to me in passing several times, took a seat on the bench facing me, looked me in the eye, and said, "I know you can do better than this." On the next examination I made the highest score in the room, and I went on to do well in the course.

Young people often act out their confusion. I was asking questions through my behavior. Are the allegations about my lack of intelligence correct? Can I do difficult work as well as my more privileged white classmates? Do I have a right to be here? The lab instructor spoke with the power and authority of the university and answered those questions in an empowering way. Many successful blacks have told me similar stories. Stanford social psychologist Claude Steele has documented this phenomenon and shown that similar minimal interventions can eliminate the differences in achievement between blacks and whites.

After my professors in a sociology course and a zoology course discovered that I was making the top scores in their classes, they began to turn to me for the correct answer, with appreciative smiles, after getting incorrect responses from other students. They took pleasure in demonstrating a black's ability to the white students. The zoology professor seemed so disappointed whenever I missed a question that I had to start actually reading the texts regularly rather than sticking to my usual habit of studying a few days before the exam!

Over the years Indiana University, like many other American universities, has done a great deal to create a sense of belonging for black students. And after a while I was able to look back with pride and appreciation, because people of good will were and are making an effort to address the issue. At the time, though, I was so confused and troubled by my experiences that I elected to go to medical school at Howard University rather than at Indiana. I reasoned that I needed to go where I was wanted rather than where I would be tolerated.

Howard, like Indiana, turned out to be a very important experience for me. I found the expected sense of belonging and comfort. There were smart black students and faculty all around me. My classes were filled with leaders. And I discovered that I'd just as soon not be a leader. I did not have to counter the myth or "carry the race." At predominantly white institutions too much of the learning motivation is a negative "I'll show them," which can create terrific pressure. Even back in eighth grade, when I made a C in mathematics I cried like a baby. I hadn't "shown them." Some of my buddies considered C a success and couldn't understand why I was upset. And the pressure to "show them" had something to do with almost straight C's during my first year of college.

The Howard experience countered my growing feeling that all the problems of the world were racial. I began to understand how complicated human behavior really is. Skin color, class, and ability were sometimes the basis for prejudice at Howard as race was elsewhere, but good social and academic performance could neutralize other differences. And there wasn't the question about whether I had a right to be there. I did not have to prove myself every day in every way to everybody. I was able to establish a positive personal identity, including my racial identity.

Both experiences—attending largely white and black schools—were important. Each led to my understanding that the race problem, while pervasive and painful, is not the underlying problem; again, it is a by-product of the struggle for power and security.

Seven years after I left Howard, I wrote an article, "The Social Power of the Negro," which was published in *Scientific American*. I pointed out historical divisions among blacks as a major reason for powerlessness and black community problems. Gus Hennenberg, then the deputy to the first black mayor of Newark, New Jersey, sent me a letter praising the article. Although he didn't add "It's the economy, stupid," he did point out that I should also pay attention to the historical absence of black capital. His comment pushed me in the direction of looking at the critical *interaction* between the individual and the institutions of the society—particularly the economic ones.

Interest in this interaction had begun when I was in the U.S. Public Health Service in Washington, D.C., six years earlier. There I observed that the black patients in the free clinic where I worked, most from the rural South, might have a second- or third-grade education, while the white patients had been through junior high or high school, some even college. For the black patients, there had generally been poor schools if any, and no support for going to school. In the District, though, you needed an education for any job that paid a living wage.

At the same time there was a daily attack on welfare recipients by Southern congressmen. Even in 1961 "welfare" and "crime" and "teen pregnancy" were code words for "blacks." I often complained that the same power structure that blamed them for not entering the job market was denying them the means to do so. But I was not acting on my concerns.

That Easter of 1962, I was having dinner in the Officers Club with my wife and young son. I was proud. I had made it. And then a group of white officers and their wives came in and shared their day with several black children from the nearby orphanage. The next day I called Nadine Winters, a black woman who had founded a "bootstrap" volunteer agency, Hospitality House, before the time of government poverty programs. It helped families that had been thrown off the welfare rolls because of minor violations. I joined and worked with other black and white middle-class volunteers over the next fifteen months.

What I experienced both at the USPHS and at Hospitality House edged me further away from the general practice of medicine. These were not deadbeat mothers who didn't care, who drank up the welfare money and neglected their kids. Most were struggling for survival by standing in line in the hot sun all day or sitting in clinics trying to get food and treatment for their children. The clinics were scattered all over town. Services were not coordinated, and there were no transportation arrangements. The mothers were ill-treated by clinic and other service personnel. Sometimes they said they had been forced to have sex to get money so that the children could eat. On one occasion when a mother broke down in tears while talking to an abusive telephone company representative, I took the phone and identified myself; he turned cooperative immediately. When I loaned one mother the money needed to get to a clinic appointment, she could hardly wait to get the money to repay me.

The greater tragedy was the children. I saw the worldly goods of one family piled on the street in front of Hospitality House as the child went off to school asking, "Momma, where will I find you this evening?" It must be very hard to concentrate in school when you're uncertain where you will stay that night. On another occasion a child staying at the refuge until his family could secure some income was found in a corner crying after lunch. He told me that his teacher said he should not come back to school if he could not bring a dime for the Easter egg hunt. I gave him a dime and sent him back to school, but I had to wonder about that teacher.

I often sat on the back stairs of Hospitality House and talked with the kids, usually seven or eight years old. They were articulate, bright, and hopeful. I thought of how different my own childhood had been and of my friends who had gone downhill from better situations than these youngsters. The economy was changing rapidly, and these kids were being left behind. There was a day labor pickup site in the neighborhood where bare-chested black men stood in the steaming sun hoping to be selected by the white contractor for that day's work, a scene reminiscent of a slave auction. I realized that unless these kids got a good education, they were headed for that labor market or unemployment or worse. The schooling they were getting was not good—even when the schools themselves were not so bad—because their family situations could not prepare them to benefit.

During my term in Washington, I decided to go back to school myself—to the University of Michigan School of

Public Health, to learn more about institutions and organizations and the way they should promote public well-being. Epidemiology caught my interest and provided me with the tools needed to put my experiences together and begin to understand why some people were underachieving and why institutions and structures were contributing to under-achievement rather than promoting success.

Human ecology had not yet emerged as a discipline, but I saw a parallel between the physical and the social environment, between the disease process and behavior. Beginning to learn something about organizations and their impact, I needed to learn more about *people*. This need led me to a fellowship in psychiatry at the Yale University School of Medicine.

At Yale we studied the internal or individual determinants of behavior almost exclusively, but what most intrigued me was the power of milieu therapy, in our case a psychiatry ward run like a community. While such short-term experiences have limited effects, the importance of constructive peers and structures—rules, procedures, authority, expectations, etc.—was clear. I extrapolated the effects to larger societal structures and considered their powerful positive and negative impacts on human behavior. I recognized how greatly my own background had contributed to my success. The problems of adulthood appeared to be rooted in childhood. And so I came to the practice of child psychiatry.

Some of my experiences with child patients have been lastingly instructive. I later realized that these incidents were powerful because they were expressions of very basic human needs and feelings.

On the power of relationships: A highly active, unmanageable child of eight years threatened to throw paint on me during a play therapy session. My supervisor observed that the child liked me and suggested that next time I tell her that if she threw that paint at me, I would be so mad that I wouldn't want to play with her. I couldn't imagine that this would have an effect on this wild child, but, needing to protect my only good suit, I did it. I was amazed that she slowly lowered the can and didn't try that again.

On the importance of belonging: A child of nine years had a surname different from his siblings born later to his mother and stepfather. His anxieties led to school and behavior problems. When I suggested that it must be painful to have a different name and to worry about belonging, he jumped up and ran out of the treatment room, seething with anger, and went, with me behind him, through much of the hospital complex. As soon as I told his parents about his feelings, they understood the problem. After his stepfather legally adopted him and gave him his last name, the boy's behavior improved dramatically.

On needing positive parent models and mentors: I was playing Wiffle-ball catch with an eight-year-old whose father lived in the neighborhood but not at home, who frequently made and broke promises to visit, and who was sometimes drunk on the corner as the youngster passed on his way to school. When I suggested that seeing his father like that must be upsetting, he turned with tears flowing from his eyes and fired the ball at me with a speed that made me thankful it was not a hardball.

Another eight-year-old, a member of a school treatment group I was working with, met me and my eight-year-old son on the street near our home. He was pleased to see me, but then inquired about my son with an expression of envy that I will never forget. I remember thinking that these kids were of like potential, yet the difference in life outcomes would be due largely to me and my wife—just as the difference between me and my three friends a generation before was due to parents.

I wanted to stay in New Haven and do something that would help such young people, but the Public Health Service had paid for my training and I had to go to the National Institute of Mental Health. One of my tasks as a program officer at NIMH was to review applications for grants in the social problem area, where the effects of poverty among blacks was a major interest. It worried me that only proposals with a standard experimental research design had a chance of being supported—and these usually came from researchers with no knowledge of the African *or* American experience of blacks. I felt that with such lack of background knowledge and with such methodology, little could be learned or done. This was 1967–68, and there was rioting and burning in the cities after the murder of Martin Luther King Jr. Something needed to be done, and I wanted to be a part of it.

I was miserable until Dr. Albert Solnit, then director of the Yale Child Study Center, where I had trained, invited me to join the faculty and to direct a program designed to try to understand why schools were not working for poor black children and then to involve everybody in working for their improvement. Even then I knew that improving education was not enough, but it was an important beginning.

I began my school work, then, with the understanding that race was a problem but not the underlying problem. I understood that education was a part of the solution, but not all of it. My questions were "Why didn't education work for the friends of my youth, for the young people of Hospitality House, for too many of the children of New Haven and across the country?" and "What can we do about it?"

Eventually I realized that many white children, a significant number from middle-class and even affluent families, were not doing as well in school as their counterparts in some other developed countries. I now believe this can be laid to our cultural view that learning is a simple matter of intellectual capacity and will; that anybody with good intelligence can teach and everyone with good intelligence can learn, if only they make the effort.

This view has contributed to our underinvestment in the preparation and support of educators, and an educational approach that does not adequately prepare most students for life in this complex age. While all schools (and students) are affected, those serving the most vulnerable have been affected first and most adversely. My work suggests that when all aspects of schooling flow from a developmental perspective, it can be much more effective. It was this perspective that enabled our Yale Child Study Center team to help parents and school people to significantly improve our two initial project schools.

CHAPTER

3

MY WORK

On reflection, it is not surprising that my questions about the life performance of people should lead me to my work in education. Our schools are simultaneously a microcosm and a reflection of the larger society. They offer clues about what makes the society run well or badly. On the other hand, because schools are greatly influenced by what is going on in the society, improving them in any significant way inevitably requires improving the society.

I recently visited a school in the Midwest that has been implementing our School Development Program for five years. It is a wonderfully warm place, and most of the students have passed the state proficiency test despite the fact that it is not a magnet school and the children are not categorized as gifted.

Looking in on a fifth-grade graduation in an auditorium full of parents, I was struck by the applause for one student in particular, Natasha. Later, her mother and the principal hugged warmly in the hall, and both laughed about how far they had come in their relationship. Afterward, the principal told me that the mother was referring to their initial meeting. Her son Timmy had called his teacher a motherfucker. The mother, summoned to the school and told what

Timmy had said, knocked him to the floor while calling him a motherfucker!

It took a lot of work to develop the relationship the family and the school enjoyed on that happy graduation day: non-judgmental and respectful getting-to-know-each-other meetings between the family and the school people, cajoling, guiding, advising, explaining, and holding high expectations. The family still has its rough edges, but the applause for Natasha represented the whole school cheering them on.

I see school people throughout the country applying what our Yale Child Study Center team learned from trying to change two New Haven schools. The way in which schools support children like Natasha and Timmy and their families is an outgrowth of what I learned by helping a boy named Johnny.

During the first year, the "bad boy" of one of the schools, Johnny, was everybody's project. A year later, with the support of the school, he was behaving much better. But one day he began fighting in the hallway. After several teachers stopped the fight, one of them, now understanding that kids act out their feelings, said, "I wonder what's going on with him." The year before, the comment probably would have been, "That bad Johnny Jones is at it again. How does anyone expect us to teach when we have to put up with kids like that?"

Back in his classroom, the child knocked over his desk. His teacher hurried into the room, but instead of sending him to the principal for punishment, she said, "Johnny, what's the matter? What's going on?" He paused and began to cry. His father was in jail, and the youngster had been eagerly awaiting his return on a Christmas pass. Something had happened and the pass had been withdrawn. The youngster was devastated.

The teacher told Johnny that she understood how disappointed he must be, but that taking his feelings out on other people only made matters worse. She helped him write a letter to his father expressing his disappointment, recognizing his father's disappointment, and telling him how he would be looking forward to the time when he was able to come home. Now instead of being hurt and helpless, Johnny was empowered. The school became a supportive place. Johnny's academic and social performance would continue to improve greatly.

When we began our work, in 1968, many educators believed a child either had ability and was motivated, or didn't. If the student did poorly, it was his fault, nobody else's. More generous assessments by behavior professionals focused on an underachieving child's intellectual, psychological, and social impairments, but still the focus was limited to the child and, at most, his or her family and community. While my childhood experiences had told me that school performance was determined by more than that, when we began our work I was not sure what else was operating. The only way to find out was to learn about a couple of schools. Then we could try to change them so that they would work better for the students.

I held an appointment as assistant professor of psychiatry at the Yale Child Study Center, a part of the Yale University School of Medicine. The YCSC team that I directed was involved in a joint effort with the New Haven school system. The team consisted of a social worker, a psychologist, a special education teacher, and myself. The New Haven school system component was led by Samuel Nash, their director of special services. Our initial YCSC intervention team was designed to include people already at schools so that once we learned how to make schools work, districts could use existing staff and the cost would not be unreasonable.

The idea was to have two elementary schools, Simeon Baldwin (kindergarten–sixth grade) and Martin Luther King Jr. (kindergarten–fourth grade), serve as representative of the entire system so that we could intervene, learn, and apply our findings systemwide and beyond. The strategy we outlined in our proposal for funding from the Ford Foundation was for us to *become an integral part* of the two schools rather than *impose intervention* on them. With staff and parents we would begin to bring about comprehensive change.

We quickly learned that change is not easy. In fact, our start was so rocky that the parents almost threw us out. Even at the end of five years, we had to leave Baldwin School rather than fight a principal. (We replaced Baldwin with a school that had a similar profile, Katherine Brennan Elementary School.) But without a willingness to change everything and everybody in the school's social system—not only the students—important opportunities are overlooked. Research that concentrates only on isolated aspects of schooling tells you very little.

Three years passed before we had a good school climate and seven years before we had significant academic improvement. Ninety-nine percent of the students at the two schools were black, and more than 70 percent were on welfare. They had been the lowest-achieving groups in the city's thirty-three schools, and by the fourth grade were eighteen and nineteen months behind in mathematics and language arts respectively. By 1984, sixteen years later, the two schools were tied for the third and fourth highest levels of achievement on nationally standardized tests and had the best attendance in the city. Serious behavior problems had been eliminated.

■ The School Development Program's Evolution

Today the School Development Program (SDP) is a child-focused, data-directed process at work in more than 650 schools in twenty-eight states. As I describe its evolution, it may sound as if we knew what we were doing from the beginning. We didn't. Initially the project was just trying to survive. We began our work with a theoretical understanding that it was important to involve parents, community members, teachers, psychologists, social workers, and noninstructional staff members (the "stakeholders") in the process of school improvement. But we did not know how to do it.

We did know that through positive bonding between the teacher and pupil, desirable child development could take place, and we believed that with good development the students would learn. But the traditional school does not lend itself to strong positive bonding; teachers teach what they are told to teach, and students are expected to learn—if they are able. There is too little opportunity to engage students and to arouse and extend their curiosity so that they can develop a passion for learning.

We learned very quickly that nobody was deliberately a "bad guy." But bad things were happening to the children. The parents, staff, and students wanted to succeed, but some of the students were poorly prepared for the learning process of school, and the staff didn't have the training to be able to close the gap. The traditional schooling was not based on what is known about how children develop and learn. It was mechanical, with no attention paid to the interactions of the human beings, small and large, who were involved.

Traditional schools are hierarchical and authoritarian in a way that does not encourage staff cooperation. Instead of promoting a sense of "ownership" and shared responsibility for outcomes, such management promotes isolation or clique formation, blame casting, and defensiveness. Every difference can become a flashpoint—religion, race, educational level, prestige of teacher's alma mater, professional task within the school, pedagogical and child-rearing philosophies. During our first year we had sharp differences in all these areas. Adults and children struggled for power and security with much finger pointing, blaming, and student fighting.

The most vulnerable staff and parents and, particularly, students were victimized regularly. Every impairment—physical, psychological, social, intellectual—sets up a student for victimization. While staff could quit or transfer, and parents could stay away from the school, the students had to attend. And they got blamed for the effects of the dysfunctional school environment: "These kids can't learn."

Some students can learn in difficult circumstances when they receive strong support from parents or others outside the school. And a rare few can learn well under any conditions. But most students will not develop and achieve well in difficult school communities. (See chapter 7 for a discussion of specific schooling problems.)

In short, the traditional was not working. But neither did our initial efforts.

We learned that formal lectures about child development and behavior are of minimal benefit. Some of the teachers who most agreed with the *ideas* could not apply them in the classroom. One wanted to be a friend to the point that she lost her authority and her ability to help her students grow. Teacher autonomy in the instruction and curriculum areas didn't work. Some could develop instruction that was age-appropriate and that stimulated growth and learning, but too many could not. And there was no schoolwide plan they could act from. Nobody, in or outside the schools, could just make improvement take place.

Through trial and error we began to bring about the thinking, planning, and changes that evolved into the nine critical components of our present-day SDP. Eventually the stakeholders organized themselves into three teams— planning and management, mental health, and a parent group. But without well-developed management skills, school-based management teams can interact badly. To aid their work, we identified three operations or primary activities. And to prevent difficult interactions, we eventually agreed on guiding principles—again, three—that allowed everybody to work well together.

Let's start by looking at the three teams.

The School Planning and Management Team creates the vision for where the school wants to go. Teachers, instead of working on their own, profit from schoolwide collaborative

Model of the SDP Process

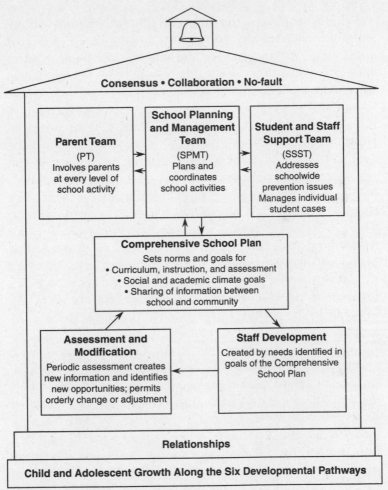

Consensus • Collaboration • No-fault

Parent Team

(PT)
Involves parents
at every level of
school activity

**School Planning
and Management
Team**

(SPMT)
Plans and
coordinates
school activities

**Student and Staff
Support Team**

(SSST)
Addresses
schoolwide
prevention issues
Manages individual
student cases

Comprehensive School Plan

Sets norms and goals for
• Curriculum, instruction, and assessment
• Social and academic climate goals
• Sharing of information between
school and community

**Assessment and
Modification**

Periodic assessment creates
new information and identifies
new opportunities; permits
orderly change or adjustment

Staff Development

Created by needs identified in
goals of the Comprehensive
School Plan

Relationships

Child and Adolescent Growth Along the Six Developmental Pathways

planning that addresses the needs of the entire school community. Each SPMT creates a comprehensive plan designed to achieve its vision and to identify and make best use of the resources already in the school.

We learned during the first years that the optimal composition of such a team is ten to fourteen people selected from and by each major group at the school. The parents select four or five members; the teachers select one representative from each grade level; the nonprofessional staff such as custodian and clerk select a member; the social worker represents the Student and Staff Support Team; and the principal is a member, usually the chair. The team meets at least once a month—usually once a week at the beginning of the year—and also whenever special issues need to be discussed.

Through the SPMT, the schools determine what change is needed and what is possible, at a speed they can manage. The team plans, communicates, and coordinates all of the many things that are going on in the school. It deals with problems or assigns them to subcommittees, and the team members identify and act on opportunities for school improvement. Because the team is representative of all adults involved in the school, all feel ownership and responsibility for the outcomes.

During our first years, the Parent Team was made up of people who came to throw us out but stayed to help us build. This team allows parents to share their knowledge about their children and the community with the staff, who in turn share their knowledge about child behavior and learning with the parents. A social worker and later a teacher worked with the parents to help them connect with and effectively support teachers and the work of the schools. Teachers and support staff would present academic and child development workshops at kaffeeklatsches planned by and for parents.

Between 1977 and 1980 we had two program components that involved parents deeply in the work of the school. The first was the selection and preparation of a parent to serve as a teacher assistant in each classroom. The second was the Social Skills Curriculum for Inner City Schools project, which helped the students develop skills that children in the mainstream already have simply from growing up in the homes and social networks of their parents.

Working in these ways has created mutual trust and a shared belief in and hope for the students. This approach creates an accountability that can't possibly be matched by rules, penalties, and the few extra dollars that merit pay brings to individual teachers—or pay for parent participation. On the other hand, pay can be useful to poor families and does not create divisiveness.

The Student and Staff Support Team (originally called the Mental Health Team but renamed to avoid pejorative overtones) is made up of the school guidance counselor, special education teacher, nurse, psychologist, social worker, and school-based health clinic representatives. The team helps the staff and the parents to foster desirable behavior in the children. This is done more by changing the culture of the school to better meet the developmental needs of children than by working directly with children. Our chief role is to help the parents and staff to understand that children are not just good or bad, smart or dumb, as their behavior might suggest. All are born underdeveloped. Some have not mastered the rules of the game, and have not had much of a chance to acquire the skills they need. When they are called upon to do what they have not been prepared to do, they may lose confidence. And they may act up.

Parents want their children to be successful, but many parents are themselves unprepared to prepare their children for school. In some cases, economic and social stress make it difficult, even when they know what to do. As a result, too many children come to school prepared for life at the playground, the housing project, and other familiar places, but not prepared for the expectations and demands of the school.

The good news is that by emphasizing child development—as opposed to control and punishment—parents and staff together can promote desirable development and be-havior. The way all the teams pull together to benefit the school and the students is demonstrated by the case of a troubled third-grader.

This eight-year-old had been traumatized and did not trust adults. She was doing minimal work and would not look at her teacher or smile. At the end of seven months with a caring, reliable, responsible teacher, she finally looked at her and smiled. The teacher, while pleased, was also distressed because in eight weeks she would have to pass the child on and would not be able to build their relationship.

The Mental Health Team held a case conference to dis-cuss this child's needs and experiences and to examine the way continuity and bonding between child and teacher sup-port social and academic growth, while the discontinuity or defective bonding in too many of our students impedes progress. The SPMT was asked to create a subcommittee, of staff and of parents selected by the parent team, to address this problem.

They came up with a plan for teachers to keep students for two years: first and second, third and fourth. The result was that some children who made no academic gain in the first year made two or more years of gain in the second year. With continuity, trust, and bonding came a willingness to open up and take the risks that academic learning requires. Because all were involved, these gains were a victory for the entire school, and the confidence building had a synergistic effect. "We can do anything. What's next?"

Now that we have seen how the teams work, let's turn to the three operations or primary activities.

The *comprehensive school plan* embodies the SPMT vision in both the social and the academic achievement areas. It uses activities that are common in some schools, like Welcome Back to School potluck suppers, book fairs, fashion shows, field trips to museums and other educational institutions, or producing and selling calendars, to create a good school climate.

Once the schools had their own comprehensive plan they were no longer forced to appear progressive by accepting every research and mini-intervention program that universities, service clubs, and others proposed—whether it was timely and useful or not. The schools engaged the outside world to help carry out their own plan. In a climate of trust, teachers began to admit that there were areas in which they could use help. This led to the teachers creating their own *staff development plan*, which in turn led to *assessment and modification* of the comprehensive school plan as new needs were identified.

Working together successfully is made possible by three guiding principles.

The *no-fault* principle: Finger pointing and faultfinding only generate defensiveness. Focusing on ways to prevent and solve problems promotes accountability.

Consensus decision making: Voting can lead to power and personality struggles that have little to do with the needs of children. There are winners, losers, and some who say, "You won, you do it." To reduce clique behavior and personality politics, we discuss what appears to be good for the children, then we go with what most think will work—with the proviso that if it doesn't, we will try the other ideas next. And in the process a better approach than any previously discussed often turns up.

Collaboration: We agree that the members of the team cannot paralyze the school principal, who has legal authority and responsibility, whether or not he heads the team. But the principal cannot ignore the considered opinions of team members. This promotes a feeling of true collaboration and responsibility for program outcomes.

With the nine elements of the SDP process in place, no teacher has to face difficult problems alone. Teachers begin to share effective practices and to contribute their thoughts to the solution of problems and exploitation of opportunities throughout the school, and all share a sense of pride with each good outcome. And yet each school, acting from the nine elements, addresses its needs in its own way.

The SDP process, when working properly, is like the chain and sprocket of a bicycle. Appropriately assembled, it allows parts that can't take you anywhere separately to be pulled together. Effort applied to the pedals now moves the system, under the control of the cyclist. With a working bike, disparate elements become more effective—curriculum, instruction, assessment, use of technology. Another way to think about it is that it incorporates many small engines of effort, which sometimes work in opposition, into a more powerful and directed engine.

In our first schools a can-do attitude gradually permeated all activities and interactions. The students now had positive models among the most meaningful people in their lives—parents and teachers. They caught the new spirit and became the carriers of the changed and ultimately desirable school culture. Thus, for example, when someone accidentally stepped on the foot of a new student, the newcomer was ready to fight. But one of his classmates said, "Hey, man, we don't do that in this school." Once he learned that he didn't have to fight his way in, he dropped his fists and also became a carrier.

The students felt comfortable and confident not only about themselves but also about the school around them. They were motivated to achieve more and to behave in a way that won them approval. That is just what had happened for me at home and in school, and for most people who are successful in school.

The makeup of the teams, the operations, the guiding principles that we evolved were based very directly on what we learned as we lived in these initial project schools, observed, and applied our knowledge of child development. The changed way of operating was responsible for the improved outcomes in the schools.

Nobody could mandate change, but collaborative self-change was possible. When staff and parents come to believe in their ability to work in this way, and to believe in the students, they search actively for opportunities to make the school work better. With each success, the staff become more open to the possibility of major changes, observing and learning from children, adjusting their program to help them develop and learn.

While we started with and still work more in elementary schools, the School Development Program is now being used in more than 150 middle and high schools. The same basic nine elements are used. But here, consistent with what we know about child development, the young people themselves are involved in school governance and activity teams. Their opinions are solicited, considered, and, when appropriate, acted upon. While they receive supervision and help in all their activities, the strategy is to give them the level of independence they can manage and hold them accountable. For example in one middle school two teachers planning a museum field trip stated their goals for the trip and enlisted the students to develop strategies to achieve those goals, with the teachers providing guidance and participating in the activity.

We now understand that the School Development Program is effective, when properly implemented, for several reasons. It provides a framework, both theoretical and practical, and the kind of structures I have described above. It provides tools and skills that teachers often do not receive elsewhere. With these they are able to systematically carry out processes that promote child development, teaching, and learning. And people with deep knowledge in these areas are available to coach and assist until the changed ways of working are internalized by individuals and schools.

■ Survival and Funding

In the early years, however, our spread and even our survival were far from assured.

The history of funding for the SDP provides some insight into the difficulty of finding support even for programs with

goals as seemingly commendable as ours—to improve the
chances of all children and of low-income minority-group
children in particular. Issues of race, conflicting theories
about how children learn in school, imperfect disseminating
of the program, and simple survival were all interrelated.

At the end of the first five years of our pilot work in New
Haven, our Ford Foundation project officer recommended
continued support. But consultants in psychiatry advised
the senior program officer that our model was unworkable.
They thought our children had psychological problems that
needed to be professionally treated, while our model assumed that most of the children were fine and the system
created the problems that needed to be addressed. The
foundation's consultants were operating from the one-to-
one treatment model—doctor and sick patient—they were
used to. We were using an interactive-systems model and
believed that improvement of school management and climate and relations among students, parents, and staff was
essential to good student social and academic performance.

We were not re-funded.

Fortunately, the staff and parents had benefited enough
from our program to save us. A school social worker, who was
preparing to take over when our YCSC team left, decided to
refer out for clinical treatment the kind of child and problem
that *teachers had been managing themselves* with our Mental
Health Team support. The teachers marched on the principal and insisted that the social worker not return. Yale Child
Study Center and Ford Foundation phase-out funds supported our work until we could find new support.

But finding another source was not easy. While the climate of the schools was greatly improved after five years, the
test scores had not moved—although everybody in the
schools knew that this was imminent. Indeed, our approach
is not specifically designed to improve test scores. It is
designed to create conditions that promote student development, adequate teaching, and in turn adequate levels of
learning.

A description of the change during the first five years, written voluntarily by a data collector just before she left to take another job, was dramatic and compelling. She described how anxious the testing had made the children in the beginning. Some could not sit still. Others would scribble in the areas where they were supposed to supply answers, sometimes pressing the pencil very hard and making dark marks. Some would cry and run out of the room. Four years later, the children were confident, cooperative, and able to concentrate on the task and respond to the questions. But they did not yet score higher, for the tests did not measure the areas in which we had made the greatest strides.

I turned to the National Institute of Mental Health, where I had served as the second-ever black professional on the staff. I tell this story reluctantly, for it will appear to be about bad people. It is not. It is an important story about organizational relationships and networking, and it illustrates the roadblocks encountered by projects addressing minority needs when minorities are not a large enough part of mainstream institutions and when the political tide turns against the poor.

Several years earlier, I had been one of the founders of the Black Psychiatrists of America. As an NIMH staff member, I had observed the way a number of grant proposals by black scholars were passed over because they did not meet the review committee's preference for experimental research design. This design tries to set up constant conditions in a control and an experimental group, and then observe the effect of one modification in the experimental group. For example, with a special curriculum, you contrast the performance of otherwise comparable students using the traditional curriculum and using the special curriculum.

Such experimental research design, however, can never address the multiple and dynamic interactions of complex systems. To the black psychiatrists, I recommended that we ask NIMH to create a minority center that would use research designs more fitted to work in the real world. Also,

having been at NIMH, I knew where the money was, so I recommended an actual operating center rather than one that
simply coordinated research activities.

An important lesson: When the Minority Center was created using some of the funds from another operating center,
a member of the center whose budget was accordingly
reduced (and who had regularly presented himself as a friend
of blacks) angrily said, "You niggers won't even know what to
do with millions of dollars!" The comment not only was racist
but, more important, it betrayed a fear of diminished control
of scarce resources, and an unwillingness to allow the less
powerful to help determine their own destiny—the approach
we used in our SDP project. It doesn't help much to call somebody a racist. But we should remember that racism is funda-
mentally about power and control.

We presented our SDP Social Skills Program proposal to
a highly qualified multiracial review panel of the Minority
Center, containing people from backgrounds that allowed
them to intuitively understand the potential of our approach—and we received support. This program had grown
out of discussions about what the children would need to
have a chance to achieve the American Dream. Parents and
staff together agreed they would need social and academic
skills in politics and government, business and economics,
health and nutrition. They would also need skills related to
spiritual and leisure-time activities.

Our work suggested that education and mental health organizations ought to be working together. But when I tried to
develop a proposal for a center that would allow us to do intervention research supported by both the National Institute of
Mental Health and the National Institute of Education, things
fell apart completely. We were not known to NIE, and too
many of the decision makers didn't understand the need for
our approach. Again, we almost lost all program support.

Around the same time, during a trip to St. Louis, I happened to run into Donald Suggs, a dentist who was a school
friend and an African-American from a background similar

to my own. Over a casual breakfast, I described our work. With no training in the behavioral or social sciences, he immediately understood the wisdom of our approach and offered arguments in support of it based on his own life and work experiences. This was not surprising, for what we were and are doing is plain common sense (or perhaps, as a colleague characterized it, *uncommon* common sense).

In connection with a subsequent application, NIMH site visitors from a traditional review panel came to New Haven to get a better sense of what we were trying to do. It was early in the 1980s, and the government was being pressured to get out of "social research." (Unfortunately, some of the pressure came from biological researchers because it would mean more resources for them.) Our parents and teachers were bursting with pride about what they had been able to accomplish. By then the all-important test scores had improved. The panel reviewers acknowledged that these were remarkable inner-city schools.

But sentiment was going against us, and one supportive reviewer, trying to be helpful, asked me to explain again whether the improved social climate was the independent or dependent variable. Several teachers looked at me in utter disbelief: What was this academic-bureaucratic gibberish all about? Another group at the NIMH was about to support us when one member of the panel reminded them that our intervention research did not conform to experimental research design. We didn't get support from them either.

We had a good proposal, an unmatched track record, good community and university support, potential for national impact, and our work was well known to the NIMH staff and reviewers. Generally, my strategy when facing a blocked door is to keep my cool and search for one that is open. But we desperately needed support, and I wasn't being treated like a member of "the club." While discussing the rejection decision with the review section chief, a friend, I blew up. He listened quietly and finally said, "I'm sorry, Jim. I think you understand."

I did. Most of the people at the NIMH wanted to support efforts to address difficult social problems. But the tide of political power was turning against minorities and the poor. This was not professional peer review, it was political action.

In 1992, a congressional committee member who heard my testimony found it incredible that we had not been able to get government support despite the fact that I was well qualified, from a low-income African-American background, with experiences and training that should have been of great interest to people trying to address problems in low-income African-American communities.

Perhaps this rejection had nothing to do with either the merits of our proposal or our approach to solving social problems. This concern was expressed by the late Ron Edmonds— and it influenced a major decision that we made. At the time Ron was on the faculty of the Harvard School of Education and was also working with the New York City school chancellor's office. Ron had detailed the conditions under which schools serving nonmainstream students were successful, and he challenged schools to create them. I was concerned that many schools would attempt to do so without being properly trained. Good ideas might be thrown out because of poor implementation. I felt that more demonstration of successful practices in the field was needed. Ron feared that there was an effort afoot in America to write off low-income and minority students. Some research then gaining attention suggested that schools couldn't make a difference, and Ron predicted it would be used to support this effort.

Meanwhile at Yale we were debating whether to seek support to follow our students over time and learn more about how to create very good schools, or whether to disseminate what we already knew, which was enough to create reasonably good schools. We decided to try for a nucleus of reasonably good schools in which young people from disadvantaged backgrounds demonstrated that they could perform well.

At that point serendipity struck twice. Bob Haggerty, then

the president of the William T. Grant Foundation, felt that it was important to support some of the programs with successful track records that the federal government would not support. Federal Judge Douglas W. Hillman heard about our work and ordered the Benton Harbor, Michigan, school district to implement it as partial settlement in a school segregation case. Between them they provided an opportunity to field-test the model—although a court order created its own set of problems.

To complicate matters, I made an error by training our first out-of-state facilitator, Erma Mitchell, for a year in New Haven. When she returned to her district, the attitude of her colleagues was "You had a wonderful sabbatical year at Yale, now you change us." The essence of the SDP process is participation and belonging. I had forgotten, or not yet fully understood, that the three most important parts of successful school change are relationships, relationships, relationships.

Benton Harbor superintendent James Hawkins visited our project schools in New Haven and became convinced that the model could work. He sent a group that was representative of all the adults involved in schools in Benton Harbor for an orientation of several days. This group experience created a bond among key people and a shared understanding. When they returned to Benton Harbor, they could create and sustain the necessary positive relationships. They were then able to make significant social and academic gains.

In several studies, we compared Benton Harbor students in SDP schools to students in non-SDP schools. The studies showed significant student gains in achievement, attendance, behavior, and overall adjustment. But Benton Harbor had serious financial problems and three superintendents in five years. Because conditions in a community affect conditions in a school, it is difficult to maintain improved levels of functioning in schools for very long without reasonable stability in the surrounding community. While some of the SDP principles continue to be used by some staff members, we no longer work with this school system.

Our second district outside Connecticut became a proto-type for our later expansion and has become the location of one of our Regional Professional Development Centers. John Murphy, then the new superintendent of the Prince George's County School District in Maryland, contacted me in 1984 about implementing our program. They had little money, so we brought Jan Stocklinski, the SDP facilitator, to New Haven for a month and had the representative group of adults join her in the last few days. They went back and began to implement the model in ten elementary schools. In three years, the ten schools showed twice the rate of academic improvement of the other district schools.

Several other districts followed, but we struggled to survive financially. Generous grants from several foundations still left us far short of what we needed to intervene on a large scale and with far less than what we had received from federal government grants. Then serendipity struck again. Hugh Price became vice president of the Rockefeller Foundation.

Hugh's father, Kline Price, was a physician and one of my teachers in medical school. Marilyn Price, Hugh's wife, was the daughter of my anatomy teacher there. I got to know them when Hugh attended law school at Yale and Marilyn was a teacher in the New Haven elementary school where I did my first work during my child-psychiatry training. Our families occasionally socialized, and we shared an interest in social problems affecting the black community.

After Hugh finished law school, he passed up lucrative opportunities and took a low-paying job as the first director of a grassroots advocacy organization, the New Haven Black Coalition. The Prices lived in a house across the street from one of our SDP schools, and their daughter was a student there. Hugh was in the audience the night we were harshly criticized and the program was almost discontinued. He watched us hang on, turn things around, and help create a good school.

He went on to gain experiences: in urban development

with a private firm; in hands-on city management on the staff of Mayor Frank Logue in New Haven; as editorial writer for the *New York Times*; as vice president of WNET-TV, the New York City public television station; and then, important to our work, as vice president of the Rockefeller Foundation, responsible for the five-million-dollar annual education portfolio. He is now president of the National Urban League.

The Rockefeller Foundation in 1990 was looking for a way to make a significant contribution to a public education universe where about $230 billion is spent annually on some 80,000 kindergarten-through-twelfth-grade schools, approximately 15,000 of which serve disadvantaged students. The Foundation sought a project that addressed what they called the gaps in the school reform movement that were identified by Secretary of Education Terrel Bell in his 1983 report *A Nation at Risk.*

The major gaps were the developmental and school-climate issues. Most current reforms focused on curriculum, instruction, assessment, and using technology. The Rockefeller Foundation strategy, like ours, was to disseminate a model that was a work in progress but not "the answer." The idea was to get a significant number of schools to *put the child first* and work entirely from this idea.

Hugh believed that our project meshed with their interests. But because of our longstanding friendship, he consulted with many people across the country besides me. The work of the SDP was widely known by now through a 1988 *Scientific American* article I had written and through many other articles and presentations over the years, and our project was repeatedly cited by the consultants as one that best met the Rockefeller Foundation's criteria.

The Rockefeller Foundation provided the first solid support we had had in ten years, and brought renewed attention to our ideas. It has enabled us to move to a model in which district-based leadership teams learn the SDP process and, in turn, help local school districts use it.

We see here between Hugh Price and myself a rare

example of an African-American old-school friendship-based mainstream network in action. But what we really need is a larger African-American network because our common experiences create essential understanding and skills, and a greater sense of urgency. The lack of such a network sometimes leads to unintended exclusion from mainstream economic participation and benefits. (I ask the reader to keep this point in mind when I discuss African-American experiences and needs in chapters 5 and 6.)

■ The School Development Program Today

Our present organization and work are still based on our pre-Rockefeller experiences, and on what we have learned as we have worked with more and more schools. Our initial strategy was to get the SDP used in a nucleus of schools that was large enough to trigger replication in many places. This is a widely accepted computer-parallel view of school reform—click, copy, move cursor, and paste. Another popular notion is that successful models will stimulate competition and the elimination of bad educational practice. On reflection, our experiences suggest that this is not the most useful way to think about large-scale school improvement.

We began expansion efforts at a nearby school in New Haven in the 1970s. The principal told me that we would not have the same success at his school as we did at our initial school, King Elementary, since that school served children from single-family homes, while his school served children from project apartments. I noted that our other school, Brennan Elementary, had improved despite the fact that its children were from project buildings, at that time with an open garbage dump nearby. He countered that those were two-story dwellings, and his school served high-rise project buildings. What he was saying was "These children can't learn."

To his credit, he did facilitate the process and help to

improve the social and academic performance of the students. On one occasion he described a staff breakfast, prepared by the male teachers for the female teachers as part of the plan to improve school climate. He glowed as he spoke. Then as a puzzled afterthought he said, "You know, it was odd. There wasn't a single discipline problem that day."

The fact is that intangibles like climate do affect behavior and performance. But many well-meaning people just don't get it. And even when they do, the skills and the courage to change can be a problem. Sometimes the teachers' employers and the community send conflicting signals—change by doing more of the same. Confused, with little support, some school staff respond to pressure for improvement with the attitude that "This too will pass." Some leaders get involved in change programs for the wrong reasons, to look progressive or to change enough to deflect criticism. In one case a chaotic school was brought under control with a child development approach. With a school the principal now enjoyed and thought he could control, he went back to the old way of doing things, and the school collapsed.

Another school district in Connecticut asked our YCSC team to intervene without designating a local person responsible for internal change. We explained why this was not likely to work but, because of their insistence and because we could learn from the experience, we agreed to do so. As expected, it didn't work. It was too easy for those who didn't want change to turn others against outsiders. We were not there for the informal exchanges and interactions that can clarify confusion and promote trust. Most important, the interest in improvement must come from a significant group of school, central office, and board leaders, and it must grow as the process is implemented. The effort must be tailored to local conditions—personnel, political, social, and economic—all of which involve hot-button issues that an outsider cannot easily grasp.

These (and factors I will discuss in chapter 7) are some of the reasons that the notion of exact replication is not very useful in thinking about creating a world-class education system nationwide. Our challenge has been to encourage schools and districts to use child development principles to improve practice through the application of the nine elements of our SDP model. Very early it became apparent that we could not expect *exact* replication. But it appeared possible for school groups to gain deep understanding, build good organizations, and apply program principles in a way tailored to a particular setting.

Our small New Haven–based staff could not manage to take us from 66 schools in 1988 to more than 650 schools in 1997. This growth was made possible through our partnerships with several schools of education, several state departments of education, and one mental health organization, Youth Guidance in Chicago, which worked with us *and* with local school districts. We have also developed a national faculty, most of whom learned to implement the SDP through the partnerships and are now an important resource pool for us.

We sought partners who could benefit from working with local school districts and would provide our program with a chance to learn about agencies that are obvious candidates for collaboration on future large-scale state and federal government school-change efforts.

In our SDP book *Rallying the Whole Village*, Louise Kaltenbaugh and Deborah Smith describe the partnership among Southern University at New Orleans, the SDP, and the New Orleans public schools. The School of Education reformed its teacher preparation program by requiring that its preservice teachers do field work in SDP schools as an integral part of their professional courses beginning in their *sophomore* year. Kaltenbaugh and Smith teamed up with Jennifer Patterson, the SDP facilitator, and Mary Thompson of the district's central office to form an educational change team. In 1993–94, a cadre of 288 university students were involved in the K-16 Partnership, working as mathematics tutors, reading assistants, speech and hearing diagnosticians, health and nutrition assistants, art enrichment assistants, and social work interns in the SDP schools.

In another example, the partnership consists of the Cleveland public schools, Cleveland State University, the Cleveland Child Guidance Center, and the Harvard Business School Club of Cleveland, whose members associate themselves with SDP schools and work with businesses surrounding the schools to foster their support.

Our partners gain SDP skills, before and after implementation in their home districts, by attending our two-week training programs in New Haven along with leaders from the local districts with whom they are collaborating. Our staff help them gain the knowledge and skill needed to coach district-based implementation teams. There is a week-long leadership academy for principals, and scheduled site visits and periodic communication between our staff and local leadership. While the training, called the Comer Project for Change in Education (CPCE) and directed by Edward Joyner, has become much more sophisticated, the focus on child development and learning through implementation of the basic nine elements of the program has not changed.

Numerous schools are using the SDP on the initiative of local people who have not received training. Interestingly enough, some of these schools have made excellent social and academic gains. Unfortunately, some show little improvement, even with training.

Some have said that our approach is helpful only for low-income, minority-group children. Until recently districts that had significant social problems and poor test scores—more often minority communities—were the most interested. But others have recognized that the SDP's mechanisms and ways of working can be helpful in preparing all young people for a more complex time, when more support for development is needed and less is available. Actually, the practices we have developed are closer to those in elite private schools than in most public schools.

The SDP is operating in school districts serving diverse

ethnic, cultural, and socioeconomic communities. Valencia
Park Elementary School in San Diego, California, serves twenty-
five different linguistic groups in an affluent area. In Seattle,
View Ridge Elementary School serves a mixture of African-
American, Asian, and white students in an upper-middle-
class residential neighborhood. In Meriden, Connecticut,
the Pulaski Elementary School's student population is predominantly white. In Guilford County, North Carolina, SDP
schools are in large and small cities, rural areas, and towns,
and the students are black and white.

■ Outcomes and Implications

In sum, our experience shows that with the SDP, schools
can be improved. And we have demonstrated that a faithful
application of the nine basic components, in which necessary organization and child development principles are em-
bedded, will produce good outcomes without cookie-cutter
conformity. I could relate innumerable anecdotes and other
indicators of success, some almost embarrassing.

One principal told me that the program probably saved
her life. When she saw I thought that was hyperbole, she
said, "No, literally." She explained that she had had a heart
attack as a new principal trying to jam change down the
throat of a resistant school community. But when she subsequently used the SDP model to share power, she helped to
bring about significant social and academic improvement
and greatly reduce her own stress level.

A previously failing school serving a housing project won
first place in the *Scholastic Magazine* mathematics scavenger
hunt contest for two years in a row, in competition with
more than a thousand schools across the country, many
middle income, some elite and private. And schools in California, Florida, Maryland, North Carolina, and elsewhere
have won state and national awards for excellence.

I recently attended the third anniversary of ten SDP

schools in Detroit. When we initiated the project in the same auditorium I saw doubt and apprehension on the faces of parents and staff. This time the enthusiasm when each participating school was announced rivaled that shown for the Detroit Pistons. I have experienced similar enthusiasm at such events in Prince George's County, Maryland, in Chicago, in San Francisco, and elsewhere. And many students in these schools are making significant social and academic gains.

Many parents have been motivated to improve their own education, employment, and lives through their involvement in our improvement process. A long distance telephone operator recognized me as the caller and introduced herself as a former King School parent. She intimated that before her work at the school she did not have the confidence to take and hold such a job. Several parents from my time of direct involvement who were once in perilous life situations have returned to school and are now successful social workers, teachers, and, in one case, a state agency executive.

Students from these low-income but no longer low-quality academic settings have earned degrees at highly competitive colleges. Some are now educators, physicians, engineers, and businesspeople. Numerous teachers and principals around the country who have been able to make the process work in their schools are now in leadership positions in their districts. Students and staff report (and reflect) better relations and motivation in middle-income areas as well.

Because policies and practices are established locally, statistical data on social and academic achievement varies in availability and comparability. Nonetheless, our director of research, Norris Haynes, has shown that students who attended SDP schools had significantly higher scores on self-concept, social competence, resilience, attendance, and academic achievement. And in less quantifiable areas, our case studies show families becoming active partners with school staff, and teachers expressing more positive perceptions of their students and collaborating more with each other following SDP implementation.

Our best approximation suggests that after three years about a third of the schools make significant social and academic improvement, a third show a modest improvement which is often difficult to sustain, and a third show no gain. Assessments by evaluators outside our program support our guesstimate.

The success of remarkable school leaders and their staffs, working alone or with our own and other national reform projects, and the approach used in elite schools show common threads: *positive school relationships; caring, responsible, predictable adults in the lives of students; a sense of belonging in constructive groups engaged in challenging learning and activities; and opportunity for students to sense direction and purpose.*

In short, many people know what it takes to improve schools. On the other hand, school improvement takes a long time, and affects too few. We expected achievement of certain goals in our initial project schools by 1973, but didn't reach that level until 1984. We did not expect our ideas to be readily accepted, but we also did not anticipate the multiple and complex problems we encountered in and beyond the schools.

Also, we know that if families and communities are functioning poorly, children cannot come to school ready to learn. We know that if teachers are not carefully selected, prepared, and supported we cannot create a world-class school system. We know that education is critical to the future of our economy and democracy. Given what we know about schooling, its importance, and the fact that almost everybody would like to improve it, why are we not making the adjustments needed?

All of this caused me to look beyond the overt and acknowledged reasons for school problems, and to take a close look at our founding myths, how they are invoked, and how they have limited the effectiveness of many community, family, and school policies and practices. I will explore the two most troublesome—intelligence and motivation, and African-Americans as losers—in the next section.

It is natural to want to hold on to the meaningful old ways of doing things, no matter how limiting—and once aware of the need for change, to try to go forth and improve opportunities for all without addressing the past. But we can't do both. The painful work of discovery and understanding of the effects of the past on all of us is needed to end our paralysis and to enable us to create policies and programs that help us achieve the Good Society that is our goal.

PART TWO

WINNERS AND LOSERS

4

THREE NETWORKS
AND A BABY

At the core of our culture stands the belief that a life outcome is determined by the individual alone. The fact that this belief is so widely held speaks to the power of the pioneer ethos. But it is a myth. When you need two keys to open a bank box and you only have one, you don't get in. The individual is one key. The opportunity structure that the society provides is the second. Developing the individual and making opportunity available is the "turning of the keys" that determines the life outcomes of individuals and, thereby, the quality of life in the society.

Every child is born into three networks that influence his or her life. Imagine these networks as three concentric circles with the child at the center encompassed by another circle which in turn lies inside a third circle. What goes on within these circles promotes or limits the development and the ultimate sense of power and security of the child at the center.

The innermost circle, the primary network, comprises the family, the extended family, their friends, and the institutions selected by them and accepting of them, such as their places of worship or fraternal organizations.

The middle circle, the secondary network, embraces services and opportunities such as the workplace, health activities, recreation, and schools. (We may consider work a human service: One's job is more than labor, since it provides personal organization and purpose.)

The last circle, the tertiary network, is the policy-making circle that includes local, regional, and national legislators and business, social, and religious leaders.

In the primary or family network, it is the heads of households (or heads of the extended family or, on occasion, of the church or club) who take the lead in interacting with secondary and tertiary networks to secure what they need to help their children to develop the capacities that *they* need—the capacities for making decisions and taking action—and the related sense of competence and confidence. These capacities grow with each success, and they are diminished or even lost with persistent difficulties. The process of growth, strongest throughout childhood, in fact continues over a lifetime, ideally producing an individual capable of acting independently, yet open to helping others and to accepting help from others.

All of the networks are affected by culture—that set of beliefs and attitudes and regular ways of behaving on both the economic front and the aesthetic, that a group creates in its effort to thrive, to solve problems, and to find meaning and direction in life. Beliefs and attitudes that are pervasive may help or interfere with the functioning of the first network, the family. Cultural continuity and adaptive change from one generation to the next are both needed for a group and a society to have a good chance to function well.

We must consider how culture impinges on families and individuals—particularly as they confront the major family responsibility, the raising of their children.

■ The Baby and the First Network

Babies are born totally dependent and yet by eighteen years of age they need to be able to carry out all adult tasks and responsibilities. They need to continue to learn, work, live in families, rear children if they choose, and become responsible citizens. They are born with only biological and behavioral potentials (including a capacity for relationship) and aggressive and survival energies. The aggressive or survival energy can be destructive unless it is channeled and brought under the child's personal control. The relationship capacity makes it possible for caretakers to protect children from themselves and others—to limit their destructive potentials. The child's positive biological and behavioral potentials must be developed by all of the adults and institutions in the three networks of influence into which babies are born.

As parents of newborns hold and talk to them, a warm feeling begins to develop between the parent and the child. The parents take care of the child's food, clothing, safety, and comfort needs. The physical and language connection, emotional warmth, and comfort reduce the trauma of birth. Such care begins to produce what will eventually become a deep-seated inner sense of security and well-being in the child. "I am" begins here.

Children are programmed to seek attention and to please the caretaker. It is a beneficial survival arrangement—but means that children are vulnerable when caretakers are not functioning well. As caretakers tend to the needs of their children, an emotional bond develops—particularly to mothers but now more and more to fathers as well. When the bond is adequately developed, its power enables parents to help the children grow.

Being a baby is like wandering in the north woods without a map, survival skills, or tools. In the beginning the baby relies completely on the parents. For this reason the very small child will not let the source of comfort out of sight and becomes one with the caretaker until growing confidence and competence permit a very slow movement toward independence. Meanwhile the child experiences both gratitude for the support and resentment that the support is necessary.

The child's sense of self begins with the simplest of accomplishments. When a child first crawls, walks, and talks, attentive parents carry on as if the little one has made an earthshaking breakthrough. Children crave this, and they want to explore more and do everything their developing bodies will permit them to do—for their own pleasure and for the approval it brings them from the primary adults. They are excited about the world around them, and they probe and explore it relentlessly. As they explore, they jabber to themselves, pull on electric cords, touch hot stoves, run, and burst into laughter without apparent reason.

A knowledgeable parent knows when to encourage them and when to limit them in a way that does not turn off the interest but does keep them from harm. This enables children to learn the rules of the social interaction games—to learn to meet their own needs without compromising the rights and needs of others. Parents who see the significance of the jabbering will jabber back, and add words. Those who ignore it, or consider it strange and tell the child to stop, will delay and limit the child's language formation and thinking.

Reading is critically important as a platform for future learning. Parents who recognize this begin to read to their children at an early age; some even do this before their child's birth (which is not totally wacky, for at least it puts the parent in the right frame of mind). Often when a father reads to a little girl at the end of a busy day, it is the only time she gets him all to herself. She may curl up in his lap, sometimes in the fetal position with thumb in mouth. The reading experience has a positive emotional charge. My siblings and I pressed close to our mother, who could barely read, and had her read the funny papers over several times to prolong the closeness.

Many children's stories have themes like "Where are you, Mommy?" These stories deal with helplessness, fear of abandonment, and the craving for security. Because these stories help children deal with being in a great big frightening world without much going for them, they want to hear them over and over. Eventually they memorize the words associated with the pictures and begin to read from memory. We adults act like fools about the level of competence they are displaying, call Mom and Grandma to tell them about the little genius. The children are pleased that we powerful adults are pleased, and they are motivated to master reading and every other task around. Thus, learning and performing at a desirable level grow first out of a caring relationship with a parent.

Children notice that parents start at the corner of the page and read from left to right, from the top down, and that they exclaim in certain ways. All of these observations provide them with prereading skills. With attention to letters, sounds, words, and sentences, some learn to read before going to school or are prepared to learn to read when they enter school.

A vivid memory of the beauty of the parent as teacher sticks out in my mind. A three-year-old peeked his head out of the open window of his car and asked his mother, who was filling the tank with gas, what she was doing. She explained that she was giving the car some breakfast, just as he had had breakfast a short while ago. She went on to explain how food provides the energy he needs to run and play, just as gas provides the energy the car needs to run. You could almost see the child's brain turning as he listened intently and pondered the lesson. Because she so intentionally passed on higher-order thinking skills in that little exchange, I asked if she was a teacher. She replied, "No, just a mom." How could this process have been different? The child could have simply been told "I'm getting gas" or, worse, "Close that window and don't bother me."

I witnessed another youngster about the same age who strayed from the checkout counter at a store, stepped on the electronic mat that opened the door nearby, and jumped back in alarm. She looked in amazement, apparently formed the hypothesis that the door and mat were related in some way, and began to test it by stepping on and off the mat. Her mother noted the experimentation, recognized it as a learning opportunity, and began to raise questions and give explanations about how it worked. The little girl walked out of the store with her mother, smiling, arms swinging in the joy of discovery. These little revelations create competence and confidence that foster success in future tasks.

An academic colleague told me of the great pleasure his twenty-month-old gains from deliberately playing a game by his own rules, even though he knows the way it is supposed to be played—showing that the thrust for autonomy and control is innate. Another told of his four-year-old spelling a word and requiring him to say it as he had asked the child in the past. Who is in charge, anyway?

Learning also comes from negative experiences. A three-year-old, furious with her seven-year-old brother who had been teasing her, grabbed a carving knife off the table and started toward him. Her father caught and held her, calmed her down, and explained in a firm but nonpunitive and nonjudgmental way that such behavior was wrong and would not be allowed, ever! Father, daughter, and son talked about better ways to get along and how to handle disputes.

Young children scream, bite, scratch, and do whatever is necessary to manage fear and insecurity of all kinds—from hunger and abandonment to big brothers who bother them. The aggressive energy of the would-be knifer was not bad or immoral; it was not even deep anger or hatred. Aggressive energy is required for human survival. But it needs modification and management in civilized societies. The father protected the child from her own destructive impulse. By taking the matter seriously and helping the children to discuss appropriate behavior, he encouraged self-control and constructive problem solving. By seeing a child as in need of help—not a demon—he minimized the likelihood of defensive resentment, the repression of a necessary level of assertiveness, and harmful feelings about self.

As cute as they are, babies are not civilized. Indeed, they have murderous potentials. They do not know the drill or have the skills to play the game of life. They will hit and ignore rules to meet their own needs. For instance, I saw a three-year-old go to the head of a line for the airplane toilet. His father explained that he had to wait his turn. Similar explanations must be given over and over.

Socializing children is a long, tough journey. But somebody has to do it. For this reason, it is important for children to be born into a family in which they are wanted. And parents must have the resources and skills to help their children develop.

The willingness and ability of adults to promote development are influenced greatly by their own life experiences. Parents with a reasonable hope of a stable job are usually best able to manage the child-rearing task. The parents of the three-year-old would-be knifer were well educated and employed. The successful and secure fathers mentioned above could take great pleasure in the autonomy, identity, and control efforts of their children, as the children gained power and confidence. Even among people without a reasonable chance of a decent job, some find security and skill through religion or in other ways.

But parents under economic, social, and psychological stress—parents with less access to opportunities—more often have difficulties with children. Despite good intentions and sometimes remarkable efforts, their care of children more often ranges from marginal to abusive. "I am" starts here, too. Sustained bad care eventually leads to a deep-seated inner sense of insecurity and inadequacy, emotional pain, and a troublesome sense of self.

I observed a nine-year-old child at an airport who had accompanied his mother and siblings to welcome a relative home. In the bright spirit of inquiry, maybe teasing because he knew better, he wondered aloud what would happen if he told the guards at the metal detector that he had a gun. His mother angrily said, "Shut up or I'll smack you in the mouth." The look of curiosity and fun fell, and he moved to the back of the group, crushed. There was no patient lesson about appropriate time and place or harmful consequences. The child just got put down and controlled.

In the office of my optometrist in a low-income area, a very large woman tried to get her bright-eyed, playful, provocative son to sit in his chair. He was humming, exploring, enjoying himself. He maneuvered just outside the range of her chair. But when he moved too close, in a flash she snatched him and slapped him to the ground with one powerful blow. Shocked and angered, I almost violated my rule that I not wear my professional hat in public. The doctor told me that the woman had been his patient since childhood. He told me of the abuse and anger she had endured as a child, and was inflicting in turn on her child. The mother clearly did not have high expectations for her child. But to my eyes this was a smart little rascal. For reasons that have nothing to do with intelligence, punitive behavior is the more frequent approach of less-educated people. Again, the problem is culturally based.

Part of our religious heritage is the belief that the individual is born bad and is not capable of desirable behavior without punishment, control, and, some believe, redemption. Others view lack of self-control as unnatural and willful. Parents and other authority figures impose control, but external control does not help the young person gain inner or personal control.

An example of this widespread belief can be seen in a former neighbor of mine who was working as a guard in a high school. When she was told that I had written an article saying it was not necessary to spank children and that I did not spank my own children, she responded, "Oh, I know that's not true. He was my neighbor and I knew his children. They were very good children."

Relying on punishment and control rather than discussion and support for responsible behavior tend to limit the exploration of ideas and independent thinking. Young people who can't examine ideas may be misled by opportunists and hatemongers. The capacity for independent thinking can best be developed in a child-rearing process that promotes inner control. It requires a gradual allowance of greater freedom and participation in decision making for children as they demonstrate their ability to make good decisions and manage increased freedom responsibly.

The outcomes of the different expectations and child-rearing styles are predictable. The father quizzed by his four-year-old daughter told how her pediatrician had examined her motor control when she was three years old by asking her to write her name in his book and read to him. Given the quality of the child-rearing experience she was receiving, he assumed that she might already be able to do so. The child's mother, a teacher in a low-income community, told of a seven-year-old in her school who had not mastered his ABC's, but his mother could not see that she should be concerned. The child was able, but had not had the preparation needed. And that youngster slammed to the floor in the eye doctor's office, though intelligent, is having serious behavior and learning problems in school.

My colleagues are academics, and our children grow up surrounded by books, discussions, artistic interests and expressions. We provide a home experience that gives our children the skills they will need in school, as do many families of business and professional people. Many less affluent or less educated families also give their children a rich experience at home. And even when the preschool preparation is not rich, many children's experience puts them above the threshold needed to perform adequately. In a good school, some will excel. But too many schools can't help the underdeveloped.

■ The Family in the Three Networks

Parents are the carriers of the culture of the networks to which they feel attachment. When they are not part of the mainstream culture, the traditions in these networks can be very different—yet just as meaningful and influential. As parents care for their children, they pass on this culture.

We underestimate the force of the process. Children are in a powerless state in which knowledge and security come from people to whom they are strongly attached emotionally. It takes an unusual effort for a child to be different from the surrounding people and culture. For these reasons immediate networks greatly affect the future performance of the developing child.

This is particularly the case when opportunities to enter the mainstream culture appear blocked. When an "outsider" has nobody to identify with, it is difficult to connect. That is why some of the students I grew up with did well in school but not after graduation.

My working-class family was poor and low-status in the steel-mill town I grew up in in the 1950s, but still was mainstream. The same was true of our Baptist church. There were models of nonmainstream cultural behaviors all around as well. Participation in both was possible for me. But a time came when nonmainstream activities precluded participation in the mainstream. That's when parental standards and expectations and my own emerging personal ones came to the fore.

When I displayed certain behavior, my mother would say, "You can't do that. You are a Comer." Being a Comer meant having mainstream aspirations—without disparaging those who did not. It meant not doing things that were illegal, not engaging in irresponsible sexual behavior.

I remember once when a bare-chested neighbor offered me a cold beer on a hot day, and I declined. We were standing in front of the employment office of the steel mill. My parents knew the personnel officer, and my mother had used this contact to get me and my brothers summer jobs. Beer drinking in public was not acceptable mainstream behavior in the 1950s. It could influence future employment, particularly in hard times when hard choices are made. Yet that evening I had a beer with that same neighbor in his home. Kin and friend can live next door or even in the same house but identify with different cultures.

Actually, I had learned this lesson much earlier. When I was eleven, I was about to "libe ate" a magazine in the neighborhood drugstore. Suddenly I looked up and saw I was being observed by a high school friend. My brothers and I played basketball with his younger brother in his family's indoor gym. My mother had worked as a domestic in that home also. If I could steal in the store, I could do it in their home. The magazine remained where it was.

On another occasion, when an opportunity to have sex was offered, I left because it was after my curfew and I knew my father would be out looking for me. I met him on my way home. He did not ask what I was up to. But as he did with all suspicious infractions, he reminded me that if I wanted to be respected and achieve my goals, there were some things I just could not do.

My father's method is important to note. He did not scold or punish. He helped me become responsible for my own good behavior. And every storekeeper, neighbor, or teacher would contact my parents if my behavior was not acceptable. The concerns of my parents and the immediate community were demonstrations of love. It is this concern that promotes honesty, decency, motivation to achieve, and self-reliance.

■ The Child and the Second Network

By school age, or five years, good child rearing should have led to significant thought and language development, and to desirable social skills, ethical foundations, and emotional development.

During the next period, between five and twelve years, young people should develop a desire to bring tasks to completion. They should gradually become able to manage their aggressive and sexual impulses in acceptable ways. Learning should become both a habit and a passion, channeling much aggressive energy that otherwise can lead to behavior problems, undermining competence and confidence in the following period—a time already complicated by puberty around age twelve.

For most mainstream children, meeting these tasks through the school is simply a continuation of a process begun at home. For students from families marginal to the mainstream culture, this stage is fraught with pitfalls. Lacking home experiences that prepare them to meet the expectations of the school, some children are made anxious by the challenges of these tasks. When they don't experience success, they feel frustrated and, as a result, sometimes act up in troublesome ways. Many eventually drop out of school or perform far below their potential.

Many children have learned to fight because they have not been taught to negotiate for what they want. Some have been told that they will get a beating at home if they don't fight when they are challenged—a catch-22 that only gets them into trouble at school. Teachers too often punish them and hold low expectations for them rather than help them grow along developmental pathways where most mainstream parents have led their children before school.

Unprepared but otherwise good children respond to punishment by fighting back, particularly when the relationship between the teacher and child is not positive. They fight for power and control through teasing and provocation, just as mainstream children do. The struggle is for the same prize— autonomy and identity. The usual response at school is to clamp down on the children. Most parents—because they view their role as protectors, and because children are extensions of themselves—will support their children. A teacher-and-school versus child-and-parent faceoff ensues, eventually creating difficulties for all involved.

In such struggles children sometimes gain mastery of skills that are self-defeating in the long run, such as manipulation, dishonesty, and ignoring the rights of others. I have seen extreme situations in which children won the power struggle with ineffective parents, then, unprotected, became frightened by their own dangerous impulses and eventually became psychotic.

Some children respond in an opposite way: self-doubt grows and they give up and withdraw. Afraid to take risks, they shun the mental exploration they need for academic achievement. These students are often neglected while teachers attend to more vociferous kids. If they are as timid socially as academically, they are also neglected by their peers, increasing their sense of isolation. Yet some of the same children can be very active and successful on the playground, in the community, and eventually in a gang or any situation they feel comfortable in. They have merely been turned off by school.

These children are still in the north woods, without a map, survival skills, or tools. Most will not continue to develop so as to achieve their social and academic potential. Most go on a downhill course and repeat the marginal experience of their parents, despite the fact that almost all parents want their children to succeed in school and in life.

When are the first signs of this disillusionment?

Because children are children and want adult approval, most of these underprepared students do not immediately challenge the teacher or reject the school program. They come to school lagging in their development compared with mainstream children, but begin to make attachments to teachers and school. They begin to develop and learn. But several factors contribute to their leveling off around the third or fourth grade.

This is when the academic demands of the school begin to outstrip the preschool and early school development of many children. The child who was helped to think about the similarity between gas and food is well into a higher order of thinking by this time. The child who was knocked to the floor, who possibly had the same intellectual potential, has very likely not developed abstract thinking and other higher-order skills. He probably can't read or handle numbers very well. But reading and arithmetic are the key to future school and work success.

Also at this time, children begin to place themselves in the scheme of things—who and what they are, what's possible and what's not. For example, I knew an eight-year-old who heard a fire engine and declared that he wanted to be a fireman. His father discussed what being a fireman was about, but did not disparage the idea. Four years later, when the youngster brought home a brochure outlining the kind of academic program that was required for various careers, the father said, "Let's see what kind of courses you will need to become a fireman." The youngster looked at him as if he had lost his mind. Being a fireman is a respectable position. But the youngster's self-assessment had reached the point where he had entirely different career expectations.

Children who are not doing well in school, or whose families are not well connected to the mainstream, view themselves as different from those in it—their teachers and fellow students with higher levels of achievement. When called on to achieve, they are being asked, in a very real sense, to be different from their parents and their own network culture. This eventually becomes a serious identity problem that must be worked through if they are to move into the mainstream culture.

Another developmental phenomenon greatly affects performance of children from all backgrounds. As young people seek belonging beyond their family, their group becomes a significant factor. This is a special challenge for children and families from groups that are scapegoated in a society. From the age when a child can be taught to value his difference— say, two or three—parents should help their children identify with truly positive aspects of their group, and to understand and manage outside antagonisms. Otherwise they risk internalizing the negative message—inferior intelligence, criminal, irresponsible—that they will pick up from many sources. My parents provided the positive message, and yet it was almost not enough to protect me from antagonisms in college when I was beyond the protective networks of home, local school, and church community. Some young people attempt to detoxify the negative by adopting those very attitudes and behaviors as an expression of their racial identity—and by rejecting all mainstream attitudes, language, activities, and people. While this response is intended to be protective, it can create patterns of academic and behavioral deficiency that only lead to a sense of powerlessness and victimization rather than effective coping.

I was pleased to see basketball superstar Michael Jordan as the superhero in the film *Space Jam*, in a theater full of kids of all backgrounds. It is a long way from *Little Eight Ball*, the depiction of a not too smart black kid with a billiard-ball head that was the cartoon I had to watch at the movies. But a full and plentiful range of positive African-American images is still missing. Confidence, competence, attachment to mainstream people and activities can be permanently limited without such images and good support for development.

Yet some studies show that 85 percent of black parents never talk about racial identity with their children. When race is mentioned it is often in angry responses to unfair situations or in extreme efforts to establish positive identity. Sometimes race as a problem is denied in order to reduce discomfort. A white colleague reported that black parents she interviewed initially denied any racial problems in their immediate lives, but after trust was established, they pointed to numerous such problems.

Also, belonging requires living up to peer (particularly clique and gang) expectations. Students who are frustrated and losing confidence are more likely to be involved with peer groups that do not value academic learning and in which they can experience belonging by engaging in behavior that is provocative.

Both the children who make waves and the ones who withdraw become candidates for problem behaviors of all kinds. Insecurities and fears that lead to smoking, drug use, depression, violence, vandalism, early sexual involvement, and pregnancy have some roots in early school difficulties. School difficulties and unmet needs—particularly a sense of belonging—contribute to gang membership.

Some student misbehavior is simply a tactic to drive people away so that they won't discover learning problems. That was the case when I was asked to see a fourth-grade student who was hostile and would not do his work. He was using the hostility to cover up the fact that he could not read.

When enough students are not succeeding in a school, a negative environment generates and reinforces bad behavior, despite the fact that most students would like better conditions. Students doing well academically are more likely to become a part of peer groups that support desirable social performance. This is the case even in difficult school environments. Nonetheless, in high stress areas, more severe conditions operate to limit preteen achievement.

■ The Adolescent in the Second Network

Adolescence, increasingly since midcentury, has become a special challenge for all. The body and mind are changing rapidly, howling for independence and self-expression in and beyond the family. But the reality for most adolescents is continued dependence on parents and limited opportunities for self-expression. Most have not had the experiences or acquired the judgment that will enable them to handle the complexities of this age. That is why an intelligent child can do the dumbest things.

While a teenager longs for independence from the family, the thought of it is also frightening. But such fear is unacceptable, so it is covered up by denial and bravado, exaggerated pressure for independence, and a pose of invincibility that can lead to trouble. The predicament of the adolescent requires a reduction in size of the parent—often taking the form of verbal attacks, belittling judgment, resisting advice.

When I was a teenager, a policeman who was a family friend stopped me outside a dangerous "dive" and advised me not to go in. I politely thanked him for his advice. As soon as he left, I went in to see what it was that these adults were trying to keep me away from. In East Chicago in the 1950s, that was not a problematic decision. In East Chicago and many other places in the 1990s, it could turn out to be troublesome indeed.

The behavior is no less challenging to parents and teachers. Provocative moves to gain power at this age can seem more like insolence than they did when children were younger. Teenage delight in new gains often comes at a time when many parents feel a loss of their edge. I remember that it took a lot for me to be happy when my thirteen-year-old son beat me in a billiards game for the first time, even though I had been promising him that his time would come. Was I—protector, provider, leader—slowing down? Was my charge overtaking me?

Teachers and parents who understand the turmoil and are secure enough themselves can go with the flow. They don't take the attacks on themselves personally. In ways that work best for each individual, they provide support and maintain desirable standards by cajoling, encouraging, paying attention, being available. They support as much independence as the young persons can manage in a responsible way—but won't hesitate to reduce it when they can't manage it, while promising greater independence again when they can.

Such parents and teachers are promoting inner control, motivation, direction, and responsibility for self and concern for others. This is very important today with all the new technological developments. Because information often comes from TV, the Internet, or other outside sources rather than from parents, teachers, or close community people, young persons must be prepared to understand their world and, without parental presence, do the right thing. They must be ready to meet their own needs and avoid exploitation of and by others.

Parenting is tough work, and some parents don't have adequate resources and support. We are all busy. So some parents listen to "I don't need you" and just retreat. They let the school or somebody else attend to their teenagers. But children need parents more than ever during adolescence. They say "go away," but they don't mean far away. They just need a little extra space. More than a few teens have resisted negative peer pressure with "My mother would kill me if I did that."

Nonetheless, many parents do retreat when their children need them the most, even in affluent areas. It is difficult to get a parking space on parent night at school during the elementary years. Parking space is no problem in middle school. By high school the parking lot is almost empty.

It is more difficult for parents under economic and social stress to go with the flow and to hang in there all the way. As a society we have done very little to address the special challenge of adolescence. For many mainstream young people, activities that support desirable development are built into the family and school life. This is the age, before the adolescent can drive, when parents carpool them almost nonstop from swimming to drama to music lessons. Most successful elite schools pay great attention to activities that allow student expression. Some youth activities are tied to private religious and social organizations. Family business and vacation activities expose mainstream young people to experiences that promote their development.

Less is provided for nonmainstream young people. Many believe that volunteer organizations should do this. And they try, but even here there is much more available for mainstream middle-income young people. I co-chaired the Carnegie Corporation Task Force on Youth Development and Community Programs with Wilma Tisch, a prominent community organization leader. Our report, *A Matter of Time: Risk & Opportunity in the Nonschool Hours,* was released in 1993. We found there are more than 17,000 national and local youth organizations in the United States—large national and local bootstrap operations; religious, ethnic, and racial group organizations; sports, museums, public libraries, park and recreation organizations; adult service groups. The report was based on extensive interviews with young people, organization leaders, research papers, and site visits. We found that young people need and want these programs. The report states:

> Community organizations provide mentors, adults who have time to talk, to listen, and to provide mature guidance . . . facilities that provide safe havens for youth . . . approaches that foster adolescents' competence and life skills . . . often focused on the challenges of sexuality, alternatives to violence, and prevention of alcohol, tobacco and other drug use . . . opportunities for youth to be involved in community service, to address local problems, and to participate in the decisions of youth organizations . . . opportunites for public performances, rites and symbols of recognition, and reflection with others on personal and group accomplishments.

The volunteers and paid workers do a remarkable, even heroic job. But they are even less appreciated than schoolteachers. And these organizations are not adequately funded. Stability and continuity are often not possible under these circumstances. Adult workers are not given the kind of training and support they need. Because we don't think in terms of personal development, these programs are generally not tied to schools and parents to create the kind of seamless web of support for development that existed for many in the past. And most troubling, they usually are not able to reach the young people living under the greatest economic and social stress.

Much of what teenagers do in the way of recreation does not support their development. In no activity that young people are involved in—private- or public-school, religious or secular, after-school, media—do we give them adequate, systematic preparation to become responsible citizens in an open, democratic society.

Too much television consumes the out-of-school time of too many young people of all ages: about 21 percent of the waking hours of mostly unsupervised young people between nine and fourteen. By way of comparison, they spend only 31 percent of their nonsleep time in school. The amount of violence on television has become a matter of national concern. But the paucity of constructive role models and the plethora of undesirable behaviors they observe is probably more worrisome. And where community and family functioning deteriorate, the impact of television behavior burgeons. Most talk shows and other media genres focus on the extremes, which are often viewed by young people as the norm. Thus, young people have unacceptable behavior on parade without counsel of adults and responsible peers—and too many will imitate it.

A court worker in the Midwest told me a tragic story. A young teen in her custody shot and killed a friend and could not understand why the dead youngster did not get up. His ability to understand reality had not developed as quickly as his ability to act.

Am I making too much of what goes on in adolescence? I think not. What the young person experiences here will have a profound influence on the rest of life. For instance, I was so poorly coordinated until I was about thirteen years old that the outfielders in our gym class softball games would sit in the infield when I came up to bat. But suddenly things changed, and I hit a line drive that rolled all the way to the track around the field. Even now—probably when self-doubt arises—I think of that left fielder chasing the ball as I rounded third base, and I smile.

The academic, athletic, artistic, and social problems and successes of this period provide the critical competence and confidence that make mainstream participation a realistic possibility or not. It is a time when identity, discipline, and habit patterns are established in a positive or precarious way. Adult success rests heavily on the platform put in place here.

I have emphasized adolescence here as critically important, but it builds on the successful transition from home to school that takes place between the ages of three and ten. And the experiences of the first three years of life, in particular, are what make it possible for children to be ready to learn. We must pay attention to child development from birth onward. When we wait until there's teenage pregnancy, drug use, and violence and then ask what happened, we are missing the boat by a decade or more.

■ The Third Network

The way policies and practices established by business, political, and other leaders (the third network) impact the secondary and family networks can be illustrated by the changes in my hometown, East Chicago, Indiana. A former college classmate recently recalled that in the 1950s this industrial city of about 50,000 people, then about 25 percent black, produced a large number of black students who were very successful at Indiana University. Three made Phi Beta Kappa in a four-year span; many were honor roll and professional school graduates. Our African-American social fraternity was first among all fraternities in academic honors for two years and near the top for about five.

Such achievement had not occurred before and has not occurred since. In the early 1950s there were still enough jobs so that most people had enough money to pay for basic family needs. There was little community and family deterioration, and people of all economic groups attended the same schools, which were adequately supported. Though the teachers were all white, by the 1950s most were fair and encouraged all students to achieve.

The church-based mainstream black culture, which highly valued education, was still dominant. My family and church culture (primary network), like that of similar families, generated the deep-seated sense of belonging, reinforced the values and ways of the larger culture, and connected us to it. Our family was involved in a web of relationships that touched our school and workplace (secondary network) and policymakers (tertiary network) and made them work for us. An example of this is the way my parents' relationship with the employment officer at the steel foundry enabled me to get a job at seventeen despite its eighteen-minimum age policy.

Because it was a small city, before much television or long commutes from home to work, there was still a real sense of community. There was almost no random violence. The football game between the two rival high schools was a huge event. With adequate income and opportunity within reach, the city had great vitality. And even poor black kids could feel they had the chance to achieve the American Dream.

But by the 1980s, national and international economic policies led to a change in the steel industry, and the Inland Steel plant in the city gradually downsized from a high of 25,000 employees in 1978 to 8,500 today. Since the 1950s local policymakers have used land zoning, exclusion of low-income housing, and other tactics to keep the people most in need of increased family support services inside the city, while moving the most affluent to the surrounding suburbs. Consequently, much business and industry has also moved to these more affluent areas, leaving the neediest communities with weak local tax bases.

These policies affected the secondary or service network—jobs, schools, family services—and, in turn, the primary or family network. Policymakers paid little attention to the question of how to increase successful community and family functioning in the face of technological change. As a result, many families are increasingly unable to afford such basic needs as health and child care. And except for physicians, the people in the areas of human development have educations, salaries, status, and working conditions that are among the least competitive.

■ The Individual Stands Alone?

All three networks in a society must operate smoothly to create conditions and interactions that will enable families, schools, and community organizations to help children fully develop. The differences in the way the networks operated in the past and operate now is the primary cause of the differences in outcome for various young people and groups.

A positive tone is created in a society through its effort to enable families and children to function well and to sense that they belong. More than laws and punishment, caring leaders and institutions are what influence most people to do what is fair and responsible. The thought of what my parents and associates would think about me, and in turn of what I would think about myself, was what enabled me generally to do the right thing. Although we live in more complex times, the dynamic that contributes most to desirable behavior remains the same. Societies that don't work to promote positive community, child, and family functioning will permit its opposite to take root.

Children who have a caring developmental experience have a good chance of becoming winners able to meet their adult responsibilities. And children who have a difficult developmental experience have a good chance of becoming losers. The quality of development of my children affects what happens to you and your children, and vice versa. So there is a need for concern among all about all our children.

Some individuals can function adequately even when the three networks of influence work against them during their developmental years. Such people are the American ideal, but they are rare. My mother was such a person. Most of us are what we are by virtue of the support for development we received, our opportunity structure, our own effort, and—very important—good luck. A modern society probably cannot thrive for long with conditions that require exceptional performance from large numbers of people who have not had reasonably adequate developmental experiences.

Contrary to our First Myth, differences in the opportunity structure created by policies and behaviors in all three networks affect outcomes. Mainstream young people are favored in every way, and this failure to support the development of other young people hurts society. Some who are the products of favorable conditions in all three networks feel they made it on their own, or are more entitled anyway. As the myth of intelligence-and-motivation continues to be passed on from one generation to the next, it becomes more and more difficult to create the opportunity structures needed by all.

In the Club Room of the Ritz-Carlton in Palm Springs a young man of privilege who looked to be about fifteen years old read a *USA Today* story on social programs and announced grandly, "I am against all social programs." In keeping with my policy of not wearing my professional hat in public, this son of Hugh and Maggie had to leave and take a long walk.

CHAPTER
5

RISING TIDES
AND TIED BOATS

Several years ago a very successful African-American medical student came into my office in tears. She was upset because one of her classmates had posed The Question: "When my people got off the boat from Europe they couldn't speak English, they had no money and no help, and they made it. Why haven't your people been able to do the same?"

I explained to the student that this is actually a common refrain that reflects two myths and contributes to our inability to solve our severe national problems. The First Myth is that unless you are stupid or lazy, you can succeed—i.e., it was through individual effort that immigrants, especially Europeans, lifted themselves out of poverty and made it. The Second Myth is that few blacks did so.

On a trip to the Midwest in 1995, I was picked up by a taxi driver who was an American citizen from Nigeria, a member of the Ibo tribe. Our immediate rapport stemmed from the fact that he thought I was a fellow Ibo until I got in the cab. He told me a story about his recent life that gets to the heart of the question, What happened to your people?

He was about to attend the nursing school graduation of his wife, an American-born black woman from Alabama. But their marriage and her study of nursing almost hadn't happened at all. After several years of courtship, they hit a crisis. She was willing to work as a nurse's aide. He believed that she had the intelligence and social skills to achieve at a higher level—and that she needed to fulfill her potential for their family's sake.

When she realized that this was the only way their relationship could continue, she went to nursing school, albeit with great apprehension. She is now proud of herself and much more confident. Working part-time, she supervises some of the people she once worked with. Some are quite envious—although with confidence, support from their spouses and families, incentive, and possibly more discipline they too might improve their own situations.

The driver went on to tell me that he was in a group of twelve Ibos who were setting aside $1,000 a month to buy a cab and a medallion for each member. They had just completed their ninth purchase. I asked him how he could be sure that all would stick to the agreement, that somebody wouldn't drop out after his own interest had been served. "Oh, no," he replied. "Nobody would want our people back at home to think he was a crook. It would bring shame. Honor is important. Trust is important."

He then described a time when he was out of the country and his wife had to decide between paying bills and the monthly medallion assessment. She didn't want to pay the assessment. He insisted that she pay it, and instructed her to tell the leader of their business group about their family's financial problem and to ask for a loan. Reluctantly she did so. She received the loan immediately, and they paid it back as promptly as they could.

This family's experiences reflect the difference between an intact culture and a broken and distorted one—the cabdriver and his group facing life's challenges effectively, and the American-born wife initially showing dysfunctional behavior. Cultural continuity can make a world of difference.

Cultural disruption, severely destructive to a group and its members, can be transmitted from one generation to the next, and result in cultural distortions that become harmful in the absence of opportunities to forge new and adaptive responses. This has been the case for too many African-Americans. Likewise, when European and Asian groups have emigrated from cultures that themselves were limiting, they have not had a great degree of success in America. The ability of any ethnic group to succeed depends on conditions in the old country and the new, and on how the immigration takes place.

■ The Rising Tide

The truth is that most Americans of all ethnic backgrounds have experienced an improved quality of life over the last seventy-five years because of the rising tide of affluence generated by an industrial economy. The rising tide lifted all boats, except those tied to the bottom or caught in tangled ropes and ancient wrecks. Blacks were disproportionately in the latter category, but more whites were limited in a similar fashion than the myth acknowledges.

The nation's technology raced from the horse-and-buggy level through automobiles and propeller airplanes to jets and rockets and beyond in roughly four generations.

- The early industrial era, from the 1870s to 1900, was still more agricultural than industrial. Participation in the work force required little to no education or special training.
- The second stage, 1900 to the 1940s, was the height of the industrial age. It required only modest education and training. Those engaged in living-wage work by the 1940s had a good chance to care for themselves and their families, and to prepare their children to participate in the economy and the society during the next stage.

- The third stage, from the 1940s through the 1980s, marked the transition from the industrial era to the postindustrial or high-technology age. A high school degree became the ticket of admission to the primary job market, whether it was needed to do the actual work or not. This period required an even higher level of education or training for about a third of the work force. We entered the communication age in the 1990s. A high school degree is now not enough.

My education occurred during the industrial age, but it prepared me for the postindustrial period, the next economic era. The education that many children receive today does not prepare them even for the present.

The largest group of immigrants, 28 million, came into this country between 1865 and 1915. Most immigrant groups experienced a reasonable degree of cultural continuity. Some even had access to capital from abroad and/or the kind of cultural cohesion that made possible the accumulation of capital within ethnic communities. Their cultural continuity enabled many to undergo three stages of progressively higher educational achievement into the 1980s, in step with workforce participation demands.

By contrast, Africans who experienced slavery in America lost the benefits of a reasonably intact culture. While the sheer disruption had the most damaging consequences, there were at least four major shocks to African-Americans that were severely disorganizing and harmful, with continuing effects:

1. Disruption and loss of culture, in particular the economic and organizational aspects
2. Effects of the middle passage
3. Imposition of a slave culture
4. Release from slavery into an atmosphere of massive hostility, and denial of access to mainstream political, economic, and social structures

In short, a rigid caste system locked African-Americans out even after emancipation. Only when that system began to crack—at first in the 1940s and 1950s, but not significantly until the 1960s, when the nation was already well into the last stage of the industrial era—could they hope to catch the end of the tide that had lifted most immigrant boats over three generations. In order to participate in the mainstream economy and institutions after the 1960s, African-Americans carrying the weight of the negative effects of their experience, and facing more subtle but still significant resistance, would have to go from uneducated and unskilled to highly educated and skilled in one generation. Despite this history, many mainstream Americans insist that blacks' wounds are self-inflicted, because of either inadequate ability or inadequate effort.

This was the history I reviewed with the medical student to explain the difference between the black experience in America and the experiences of other immigrant groups. As a result, this talented, concerned student no longer felt paralyzed by the myths and would be better equipped to address problems rather than feel diminished by them.

What is most troubling here is that the black student and her white classmate are among the best educated people in America. Yet neither one of them had anything close to an understanding of the issue. No wonder our nation has not been able to limit scapegoating and address problems that threaten our future.

Let us therefore explore this powerful misperception about blacks a bit more: Why does it persist in the face of black success in every area in which the black community has encountered anything close to a level playing field? Why are problems among blacks magnified, while problems among whites are downplayed? Why are the policy-based aspects of problems among all Americans missed until they are almost out of control—until the well-being of the entire society is threatened?

■ Origins of Wealth and the Opportunity Structure

The primary wealth of this country came initially from farming, trading, and natural resources. On the rapidly developing Eastern seaboard, the most pressing need was labor. In the North, this lack was filled by indentured servants, serfs, and slaves, usually one or only a few to an owner. So pervasive were these forms of servitude that Henry Pelling, an authority on labor history, has estimated that at the end of the colonial period, over half the white population belonged to these three groups. Yet in colonial and early America there were also many self-sufficient farmers. Blacks were introduced into the colonies in 1619, probably as indentured servants at first, and in increasing numbers after 1730 as slaves.

In the Chesapeake Bay area, and then farther south, the explosive early growth of the tobacco industry favored the creation of plantations. Soon the owners turned to brutal forced labor to achieve their goals. At first the workers were mostly young male indentured servants and slaves drawn from Native Americans, English convicts and orphans, and Africans. Some of these men were branded or mutilated for work and social transgressions, and many were whipped when they didn't meet quotas. It is estimated that two-thirds of the indentured servants died before their term was up.

A disastrous turn for African labor followed Bacon's Rebellion against the most wealthy planters in Virginia in 1676. It was led by a modestly well-to-do planter, Nat Bacon, whose forces included other small landowners, freemen, servants, and slaves, both black and white. The terms of some of the indentured servants were ending, and this contributed to a general clamor for land among the have-nots. The elite landowners, threatened by the coalition of poor whites and slaves, felt an urgent need to destroy the powerful potential of this combination.

Prior to this, some blacks had achieved significant economic success in the North. But as a result of the Bacon rebellion, the terms of black slavery became more codified into law. A. Leon Higginbotham, in *In the Matter of Color*, has shown that a series of legal decisions in Virginia around this period, using severe penalties, took away all black rights. As Bruce Levine and his colleagues describe it in *Who Built America?*, "Through laws that placed all whites above and separate from blacks, Virginia's elites created racial bonds among whites that withstood the strains of economic and political inequality, and made it unlikely that poor whites would join blacks against their rulers." They began to end the system of indentured servitude and at the same time locked blacks into lifetime slavery.

Between the Revolutionary War and the Civil War, the federal government acquired 1.8 billion acres of land from the existing states and through the Louisiana Purchase. Most of the land was simply seized from the native population. Between 1871 and 1940, 1.1 billion acres were all but given away, largely to white males, distributed in the following ways:

- 301.8 million acres sold at low cost through public auctions under various acts such as the mining laws
- 287.3 million acres distributed via the Homestead Act
- 330.5 million acres given to the states
- 94.3 million acres granted to the railroads to encourage railroad construction
- 61 million acres granted to veterans as pension compensation
- 68 million acres granted for miscellaneous purposes

After World War II only 400 million acres of federal land remained, most of which is now designated as public lands.

I have personal knowledge that "gift land" led to political and economic power. The white Comers who held my ancestors in slavery eventually acquired great wealth and influence in business and politics. They got their start from land granted for service in the Revolutionary War.

Matthew Josephson, author of *The Robber Barons*, wrote: "The very occasion of choosing a site for a National Capitol had been the outcome of collusion between the great land-grabbers, securities speculators, and the statesmen. . . . The sequel to the Mexican War was an orgy of land-grabbing and speculation in which the origin of the war is not hard to trace." When the Illinois Central Railroad was awarded a 2.6-million-acre land grant between Chicago and Mobile, Alabama, the company heads sold chunks of land to their friends at $2.50 an acre along the line. Later the public bought it at ten to fifteen times the original price.

In these ways wealth moved from public hands (government) into private hands (individual and corporate wealth). And during the nineteenth century America was gradually transformed from a self-sufficient agricultural society to a largely industrial, commercial-consumer society. This led to the creation of powerful political, economic, and social structures, along with power elites.

As the transportation infrastructure was developed, this transformation eventually stretched across the country. The men who created the power structures were the initial source and force of the American Dream—the notion that anybody who is smart enough and works hard enough can make it big in America. And the many rags-to-riches stories added strength to this ideal.

For the poor, participation in the union movement was one way to imagine the possibility of sharing the wealth and power. And for many, the American Dream always meant simply an opportunity to earn a reasonable living, worship as they chose, and participate as a citizen.

The American Dream was not a myth. *The myth is that men who built enormous fortunes in the nineteenth century achieved their success on their own, and that everybody had the same chance.* Having access to the power structures, with occasional serendipity, was the major reason for their success.

These power networks effectively determined who could become a member of the "club" and who could not. Knowledge, skills, contacts, and information were gained in tightly woven circles of family, business, and community. All of this put insiders in the best position to take advantage of the most promising emerging opportunities, to drive future economic development, and to establish the tenor and tone of social life.

Each generation, for better or worse, built on the activities, institutions, and structures of past generations, transmitting knowledge, skills, contacts, and wealth within families or among their own kind. All groups who came later had to tap into these structures or create new ones themselves in order to gain major wealth and power, or even reasonable employment.

Andrew Carnegie, Cornelius Vanderbilt, and John D. Rockefeller are legendary figures. But the careers of George Peabody, the Morgans, and John Wanamaker span the 150 years of transformation and best show the way these economic, political, and social structures were put in place. While not typical, their work was crucial and to some extent the model for a nationwide process. Interestingly enough, aside from the later Morgans, they had little education; but they created and had access to opportunity structures.

George Peabody was born into poverty, yet with little education he went on to become a prosperous dry goods merchant in Baltimore. During a debt crisis in 1835 he was one of three commissioners sent by the state of Maryland to renegotiate state-backed loans from British banks that financed the buildup of the state's infrastructure. He threw a big party for a dozen bankers and convinced them to save their investment by investing an additional eight million dollars.

Three years later, he opened a merchant bank in London that financed and traded in dry goods and dealt only with governments, large companies, and rich people. He promoted America and American products in Europe and prospered. But in the American economic depression of the

1840s, five states defaulted on their interest payments. As a result, the reputation of America and Peabody and the value of the bonds plummeted. Undaunted, Peabody bought up the depreciated bonds, eventually helped to elect Maryland and Pennsylvania legislators who favored repayment, and made a fortune on the deal.

Peabody and others delivered European money that financed the infrastructures that helped to make the American industrial revolution possible. The rise in American economic fortunes at a time of revolutions across the European continent made America a safe money haven—and Peabody superrich and powerful.

Junius Morgan became his partner in 1854. The Morgan story (described in *The House of Morgan* by Ron Chernow) is one of movement from marginal to significant to primary wealth that spans most of American history. Miles Morgan arrived in Springfield, Massachusetts, from Wales in 1636. The Morgans were farmers until 1817 when Joseph moved to Hartford, Connecticut, and became a businessman and a powerful community leader. He bought various enterprises, directed a bank, helped finance a railroad, and was a founder of the Aetna Fire Insurance Company.

Joseph Morgan bought his son, Junius, a partnership in the dry goods company of Howe and Mather in 1836. In 1851 Junius himself bought a partnership with J. M. Beebe, forming J. M. Beebe, Morgan and Company, which exported and financed trade in cotton and other goods worldwide. Peabody turned to Beebe when he was looking for an heir, and Beebe recommended Junius. Junius built his own firm on the base of his Peabody experiences, contacts, and huge earnings.

From Junius in 1864 through J. P. Morgan Sr. to J. P. Morgan Jr.'s death in 1943, the House of Morgan grew into the most powerful private financial institution in the world. Chernow points out that they were a cross between a central bank and a private bank. They stopped panics, saved the gold standard, and helped settle financial disputes. They had great influence within the power structures of many countries, and almost all of the top hundred American corporations were their clients.

The Morgans contributed a great deal to charity, mainly to private and elite institutions such as the Metropolitan Opera House, the American Museum of Natural History, the Groton School, particular hospitals and churches. This was true of many of the leaders of the largest corporations, and their support and policymaking roles shaped the practices of elite educational and cultural institutions. But they gave little attention to problems of poverty.

The railroad expansion that the Morgans helped finance spawned service businesses of a new kind and magnitude. The business that John Wanamaker built is an example. His life and work show how business leaders influence communities and their residents. William Zulker describes his rise in *John Wanamaker: King of Merchants.*

Of Dutch and Huguenot extraction, Wanamaker was born in Philadelphia in 1838. His father owned a small brickyard in which John and his three brothers and three sisters all eventually worked turning bricks. But the coming of the railroads led to larger brickyards that crowded out the small Wanamaker yard.

Young John then went to work as an errand boy in a bookstore, earning $1.25 a week. Over the next five years he worked in two clothing stores, and in 1861 he started his own clothing store, followed by a second in 1869. Sales on opening day in his first store amounted to $24.67, the first year brought in $24,125.62, and by the end of the first decade of business annual sales for the two stores were more than two million dollars. Contracts to manufacture military and customs-guard uniforms helped during the early years. Wanamaker went on to build a sixteen-store empire.

Wanamaker stood for honesty, responsibility, and community, and his key principles became the standard of good consumer-oriented business practice: full guarantee, one price, cash payment, and cash return if dissatisfied. He introduced extensive advertising for his stores and is credited with developing the department store concept, though it appears to have developed simultaneously in Europe.

He knew how to use his community involvement to promote his business interests. A religious revival that he promoted drew huge crowds in an area that became such a popular place that he shortly thereafter located his first big store there. He was a director of the United States Centennial Celebration, attended by President U. S. Grant, and the big store in Philadelphia that made his career was so close to the centennial fairgrounds that the crowd pouring out of the fair poured into the store.

He also used his business to promote a feeling of community among his employees and in the city. He established the Wanamaker Insurance Association for employees in 1881 and was the first such store to establish a profit-sharing plan. He established an institute for the instruction of young employees, the American University of Trade and Commerce, located in his Philadelphia store, and provided two weeks of free summer vacation at his seashore camp. He opened a residence for women employees, a library, an athletic field for his company employees.

It was similar behavior by economic leaders everywhere that created the nongovernmental institutions that helped to meet needs and create opportunities for average people. These institutions fostered attitudes and values that made a sense of belonging, of community, possible.

Wanamaker contributed $25,000 to help found a YMCA for blacks, and he received an honorary degree from Howard University. But he conformed to the rigid racial caste structure that mandated a separate YMCA, and no blacks were employed in sales in his stores until after World War II. Indeed, throughout the time that American power structures were being put in place and the average white American was benefiting from their activity, blacks were either in slavery or living at the lowest level of society.

■ Black Shocks

James L. Gibbs Jr. and others in *Peoples of Africa* have provided us with a good sense of the quality of life in the West African region from which most African-Americans originally came—specifically the Gold Coast and Ivory Coast around the Niger delta and Dahomey. Life in West Africa was significantly different from life in Europe and early America, and conditions varied between West African societies, but certain structural and functional elements were essentially common. *A close-knit kinship structure was at the core of all political, economic, and social organization.* As Mannix and Cowley write:

> The communal life of many tribes was so highly organized by a system of customs, relationships, taboos, and religious ceremonies that there was practically nothing a man or a woman could do that was not prescribed by tribal law. To separate an individual from this complex system of interrelationships and suddenly place him, naked and friendless, in a completely hostile environment was in some respects a greater shock than any amount of physical brutality.

Shorn of their own culture of well-defined relationships and rewards, the African captives were particularly vulnerable to the demeaning slave culture imposed on them.

The second shock—the middle passage—was experienced by white and black slaves and indentured servants alike as the most extreme cruelty. Even white seamen were badly abused, and, as is usually the case in difficult human conditions, the abused seamen abused their human cargo. Some estimates indicate that about half of the twelve million Africans brought to the New World—of whom fifteen percent were bound for North America—died as a result of the harsh conditions of the voyage or during the brutal introduction to slavery.

In order to reduce the likelihood of rebellion among new captives and slaves, families and tribal members were often separated, to their severe psychological damage. The many reported cases of "fixed melancholy" and "madness" and suicide attest to their trauma. Some of the captives appeared to "will themselves to death" by holding their breath. This should physically not be possible. But Mannix and Cowley write, "The simplest explanation . . . is that they were in a state of shock as a result of being carried through the terrifying surf into the totally unfamiliar surroundings of the ship."

The third shock—slavery—was a system of imposed dependency and inferiority, with no opportunity to improve one's status. Slave narratives show that every function of life was subject to the will of the master. Marriage: "That's your wife." Sex: "My sister Emma was the only woman he [the master] have till he marries." Work: "Rousing the niggers to git in the fields ever 'fore light." Worship: "Old Master let him preach in the kitchen." Food: "At times they would give us enough to eat. At times they wouldn't." Clothing: "They didn't know nothing 'bout no britches till they was great big." Shelter: "Down in the quarters every black family had a one or two bedroom log cabin."

Josiah Henson escaped from slavery and told of how a white overseer had brutally attacked his mother and how his father had rushed to her defense. Slaves were summoned from surrounding plantations to witness his father's punishment of fifty lashes administered by a powerful blacksmith. From that day on, his previously good-humored and light-hearted father became sullen and morose. Finally, no longer of value, his father was sold away from the plantation. Young Henson observed the beating and abuse of his father and mother, and their total powerlessness, when he was five or six. This is an age when children identify strongly with parents, who are seen as powerful and protective.

Soon afterward, the white master died. On her knees, clutching the legs of her new master, his mother begged not to be separated from her child. The new master violently and repeatedly kicked her to disengage himself. Separated from his mother and placed in slave quarters with forty others, Henson almost died. No one provided him with emotional support, and he was only occasionally given food or drink. This was odd behavior for a people in whose past culture the responsibility of an adult for a child was sacred. But caring can be destroyed in a situation of extreme abuse and powerlessness, where concern for others is not promoted by those in power. By chance, Henson was returned to his mother, recovered rapidly, and grew to a vigorous adulthood.

A master's relations with a slave, abusive or not, are like that of an adult with a young child. The white master provided protection, defined the social role, and represented the only security a slave had. Contrary to the myth of huge plantations, most slaveholdings, particularly in the upper South, were small, about three to five slaves. This permitted tight control.

The male slave did not provide for his family. He did not go to battle in the name of the lineage, tribe, or nation. He did not return from battle as a conquering hero to be feted and honored by his people—nor could sacrifices be offered in his honor if he failed to return. He was neither farmer nor herder nor chief. Slaveholders could use any method necessary to obtain obedience. The situation sent a message to slaves that clearly told them that they had no value except as somebody's property.

There was nothing inherent in the system to promote striving for long-range goals. There could be none. Slaves derived their identity and fate from a degrading relationship with their owner, no matter how kind the master or how humane the treatment. It is understandable that many slaves looked to the master for almost everything and not to their kin or other slaves. When the slave child looked to the parents, he was taught through scolding and beating to submit to the system for his own safety.

Black children were born into these conditions for almost 250 years. This was a horrendous legacy in a country
that valued independence and pull-yourself-up-by-your-own-
bootstraps initiative.

Initially slavery was justified on the grounds that blacks
were heathens. But once the slaves became Christians, this
argument no longer worked as neatly. Blacks were now
deemed simply inferior and very different from whites.
Some planters even argued that blacks were subhuman, jus-
tifying branding and other animal-management practices.
In 1837, John C. Calhoun, a senator from South Carolina,
made a speech on the floor of the United States Senate that
held that slavery provided a heathen and inferior people
with uplifting benefits.

This kind of rationale reduced owner guilt and permitted
the denial of wrongdoing or harm. In every sphere of Southern life, early leaders transmitted a negative attitude toward
black people. It is understandable, then, that the man in the
street, hearing the words of his social betters, developed
racist attitudes. In all activities—church, election rally, labor
meeting—the message was the same: Blacks are inferior and
not entitled to the privileges of white men.

After the Civil War, poor whites who had observed the
slavery of blacks felt a sense of superiority along with a feeling that the presence of blacks denied them jobs. In reality
poor whites were being denied political, economic, educational, and social opportunities by more powerful whites.
But through identification with the broader white group,
poor whites were inclined to vent their frustrations over
inequities in their relationship with more powerful whites by
attacking blacks.

The fourth shock—the release of slaves into a hostile environment in both the North and the South—stripped the
former slave of what little protection slave masters provided
them as valued property, leaving them neither slaves nor citizens. More than 90 percent of all blacks in the country lived
in the South. The Bureau of Freedmen, Refugees, and Aban-

doned Lands, created just before the end of the Civil War, was to provide medical care and supplies, negotiate contracts between former slaves and employers, and divide and provide them with confiscated land. But the Bureau was not effective.

Having paid a high price in life and money and having lost the war and their investment in slaves, most plantation owners were hostile and intent on finding a low-cost way to maintain black labor.

Much of the political savvy and organizational know-how that the immigrants displayed grew out of a labor movement that had been gaining strength since the early part of the nineteenth century. After slavery, many immigrants and their unions blocked the newly freed blacks from working, attacked them for working as strikebreakers, and then criticized them for not working. In many places across the country, whites walked off the job when blacks were hired. Whites who cooperated with the hiring of blacks were intimidated or expelled from the unions. Mutual benefit societies recruited their own ethnic groups, joined unions, developed apprenticeship programs, and controlled access to jobs. They hired their own, sometimes even those not qualified. Some employers, for their economic benefit, deliberately created interethnic conflict. The migration of blacks out of the South was discouraged. Oregon, Indiana, and Illinois passed laws banning them.

Thus the newly freed blacks, already traumatized by the effects of slavery, now were without access to a freeman's opportunities.

The violence and abuse against blacks became so extreme that Congress had to pass the Fourteenth Amendment in 1866 making blacks citizens, which entitled them to the protection of the law without necessarily giving them the vote. After even more extreme abuse, with rising outrage in the North, Congress in 1867 passed the Reconstruction Act, which gave black men the vote and required black participation in state constitutional conventions. Federal troops were sent to enforce the new law. But even this did not enable the freedmen to compete on a level playing field with other citizens.

The Union League—a national organization formed to promote the Union effort during the war—immediately became the political action center for blacks. Through black and white organizers the Union League developed local political clubs across the South. But blacks involved in politics or trying to acquire land were sometimes denied work and sometimes subjected to violence and terror.

Nonetheless, black political participation created a public school system in the South, although it was racially segregated. And while enforcement was uneven from place to place, segregation in public accommodations was outlawed. The courts and political institutions at this time generally supported laborers in disputes and shifted the tax load to the rich. But except in South Carolina, there was almost no land reform.

Eventually the Ku Klux Klan, often led or inspired by wealthy planters, systematized the violence against blacks. They went after Union League organizers, black ministers, and blacks trying to rent or buy land. Most of the federal troops were withdrawn and protection was gone after 1869. Northern industrialists interested in improving the business climate in the South began to side with their Southern counterparts. These and other factors led to a political compromise, and Reconstruction was ended by 1876.

For a short time in the 1890s it appeared that the Populist political movement might promote black interests. Blacks, poor whites, and labor pulled together in significant numbers. Again, the power elite in both the North and South—particularly the Northern industrialists—successfully undermined this effort. By the 1890s, most of the gains made in land ownership, better working conditions, and desegregated public accommodations were taken away through violence, economic intimidation, and "legal" requirements that effectively denied blacks the vote. The use of black convicts as unpaid laborers—often men who had been arrested for vagrancy because no one would hire them—and share-cropping essentially returned the community as close to slavery as possible.

■ A Level Playing Field?

Some argue that blacks and the 28 million new immigrants that poured into the country between the end of the Civil War and 1915 had equal opportunities. While it's true that the immigrants also faced a climate of hostility, the similarity stops there. They had cultural continuity, and they had much greater economic and political opportunities.

Many immigrants came in groups from the same countries in Europe and Asia. They often settled together in the same area, drawn by friends and kin. They usually continued to worship in the same way. They were able to hold on to traditions and customs that gave meaning and direction to their lives. Although large numbers lived in ghettoes, not all of these were dysfunctional neighborhoods breeding crime and poverty. It would be more appropriate to call many of those neighborhoods homogeneous ethnic enclaves. Even in troubled neighborhoods people spoke their native language as they learned English. Cultural continuity contributed to group cohesion.

Eventually ethnic banks and other financial arrangements evolved. But in the beginning most capital came from well-functioning families who saved, pooled their resources, and worked together in family enterprises in an effort to prosper. Even now most businesses begin this way. And the families with ties to capital back in the old country and to established kin, friends, and countrymen in the new got a quicker start. Some had had experience in business in their native country.

Economic activity generated jobs and constructive social and community activity. As businesses prospered and expanded, the heads of the businesses often drew their employees from fellow countrymen. In this way new groups established their own power structures and gained access to existing structures.

The story told by Gerald D. Nash in *A. P. Giannini and the Bank of America* is a classic example of how the interaction of cultural cohesion, political and economic access, and related ethnic community-based power led to great power within the larger society.

Giannini was the son of poor, recently arrived Italian immigrants, Luigi and Virginia, who got their start managing and then buying a small hotel which served other Italian immigrants. With their earnings they bought a farm and sold produce. When Luigi was killed by an employee in a minor dispute, Virginia managed to carry on the business successfully. She remarried, to another immigrant, Lorenzo Scatena, who was a driver for a wholesale produce company. Scatena eventually established his own company and, with his sons, built it into one of the largest and most successful in San Francisco.

Aware of the benefits of good political connections, and concerned about the dampening effects of blatant corruption on legitimate business and community development, young A. P. Giannini engineered the election of a reform candidate for mayor, James D. Phelan. Giannini provided transportation and armed guards to protect the voters from "machine thugs."

He got out of the produce business and entered real estate just as the population boomed and land prices increased sharply, around the turn of the century. Then, with his stepfather, he founded the Bank of Italy in 1904. They established an aggressive loan policy to take advantage of the rapid growth of the area and to serve people they thought could become prosperous—those who were being victimized by loan sharks, and small business types who had never used banks before. Having kept the gold of many Italians in the safe in his general store because they distrusted people outside their community and had difficulty with

English and in dealing with banking institutions that showed disdain for them, Giannini was well aware of the need for a bank that could cater to such customers.

The bank was thriving when the 1906 earthquake hit. As fire spread through the city, Giannini move the bank's records, cash, and gold past looters and robbers to his home in San Mateo on horse-drawn flatbeds disguised to look as though they were carrying produce and personal belongings. Because of the intense heat other bankers couldn't get to their money and records and were unable to reopen for some time. But four days after the quake the Bank of Italy was serving its own customers, as well as those of its competitors.

Giannini's feat made him a local hero and a legend. Innovations and acquisitions, including a financial organization called the Bank of America, enabled him eventually to build a small bank—formed to meet the needs of a rejected ethnic community—into one of the nation's most powerful financial institutions. This was done with the help of a huge network of contacts in politics, friends, and emerging businesses in and outside the Italian community.

As Giannini's story illustrates, ethnic businesses, related political activity, and union-derived benefits combined to make it possible for a critical mass of people from various ethnic groups to make significant gains in one generation. Cultural continuity and cohesion contributed greatly to group political and economic power. Opportunity pulled young people into the mainstream; community and family pushed them in.

■ Education and Opportunity

Education played a key role in the development of individuals and groups and, in time, the country. Agitation for free public schools grew in the 1830s and 1840s, and educational opportunities were extended to great numbers of the poor in the North. State and local governments supported these schools. The South provided only limited education until the late 1860s.

Just as land was used to attract settlers to the West and to promote the development of railroads, so it was used to promote education. This practice occurred most in New England and was the predecessor of the federal land-grant acts. From the early 1600s land grants complemented the private endowment of schools. In 1785 Congress passed the Survey Ordinance for the disposal of lands in the Western Territory, reserving one section of every township for public school maintenance.

Before the middle of the nineteenth century, higher education was primarily classical and professional, and largely for the affluent. Such education did not reflect the interests or needs of the agrarian and industrial segments of the American society. Jonathan Baldwin Turner, a graduate of Yale and a professor at Illinois College, was a principal institutional advocate for change. He was opposed by those who argued that it was impossible to educate the industrial classes. Congressman Justin Smith Morrill was the principal architect of the Morrill Land Grant Act of 1862, which gave thirty thousand acres of federal land or the equivalent in money to each state for the establishment of colleges specializing in agriculture and the mechanical arts. Massachusetts Institute of Technology, the University of California at Berkeley, Purdue University, the University of Wisconsin, and other highly regarded institutions are land-grant colleges and universities.

State and local governments began to create free and low-cost college and university systems. New York City, California, and others built world-class universities. Only in the last decade—and at a time when more minorities are eligible—have tuition costs begun to rise significantly. Free or inexpensive land and education, along with industrial and business development, set the stage for the generations of rising fortunes in which many Americans justifiably take pride.

Ironically, black participation in Reconstruction legislatures made possible the education programs from which white Southerners later benefited and blacks were all but excluded. There is a lively debate as to whether classical education or industrial education would have served blacks best at the time.

E. Franklin Frazier pointed out in *Black Bourgeoisie* that the textile industry drove industrialization of the South, and poor whites were given the industrial education needed to work in this area. Poor whites, with the cooperation of the white owner class, prevented blacks from being employed in the industry, and from gaining mechanical skills in general.

Industrial education and employment created the broad economic base during the last part of the nineteenth century and the first half of the twentieth that lifted the white masses out of extreme poverty and provided the springboard for many to subsequently give their children the higher level of education they would need to participate in the mainstream economy in future generations.

White leaders were quite willing to provide blacks with "classical education" because it cost less. Home economics and domestic sciences were the favored industrial education courses given blacks, but it only helped them to remain a servant class. Many went into teaching instead, often without the standard preparation.

Only Virginia, Mississippi, and South Carolina used any of the first Morrill Act land-grant money for black education. The second Morrill Act in 1890 required that money be used for all, although a separate-but-equal arrangement was acceptable. But a study intended to show that conditions were improving in the 1930s showed that as late as 1936, in the seventeen states that had separate institutions, 6 percent of the funds went to land-grant colleges for blacks, who made up 23 percent of the population. In 1955 the fifty-two land-grant colleges for whites received 25.7 percent of their budgets for education and general purposes from federal funds. The seventeen black colleges received 3.1 percent.

In a study of 882 college and university endowments in 1964–65, Harvard University had an endowment of nearly $600 million; a leading black institution, my medical school alma mater, Howard University, with only a third fewer students, had an endowment of $5 million. Indeed, the combined endowment of the 106 black colleges was half the endowment of Harvard, and the combined endowment of two prestigious white women's colleges was equal to that of all the black colleges. Only three of the black institutions reported an endowment above the $9 million average of the 882 white ones.

The same disparity existed at the primary and secondary level. During the 1931–32 school year the nine states that had 80 percent of the black population of the country had a per-pupil expenditure that was from three to seven times higher for whites than for blacks. And generally, the higher the percentage of blacks in an area, the greater the disparity in per-pupil expenditures. When crops didn't do well, black schools were closed, and they were frequently closed during cotton picking season. When school boards wouldn't provide funds, black sharecroppers and tenant farmers often pooled their meager resources to hire teachers. Teachers sometimes accepted food and housing in lieu of salaries.

■ The Black Church

In the last chapter I described how social networks interact to limit or promote desirable family and individual functioning. In this chapter I have shown how the latter was the case for many white immigrants. During and after slavery, however, conditions in every network worked first against the slaves and then against the African-American community.

The adaptive slave response was the creation of a distinctive black church. Forged from remnants of West African cultures—song, dance, verbal expression, food, games, rituals—combined with aspects of Protestantism, it provided some psychic protection and social organization. It promoted desirable family functioning despite the limited income of households. It became the nucleus of African-American culture.

Blacks received help from Northern white industrialists and rich individuals, philanthropists, and religious groups. But in order to secure the fundamental human and legal rights available to most immigrants almost from the moment they stepped off the boat, a largely church-based black culture had to build the institutions, lift the social conditions of many, and create the leadership needed to effectively challenge Jim Crow conditions. Self-help was the answer. Indeed, almost 20 percent of the six million dollars used to set up four thousand schools for freedmen came from the black community itself.

■ Accessing the Economic Opportunity Structure

While cultural continuity, cohesion, power, respect, and trust enabled other groups to overcome resistance, these were precisely the conditions that the four shocks denied blacks. This, combined with their low caste designation, made access much more difficult for them.

The proceedings of the meetings of the National Black Business Association, founded in 1897 and continued over a couple of decades, show that African-Americans looked to business to lift the masses, build cohesion and community, and support family functioning. Slavery had demeaned work, and leaders believed this could be changed through freemen working in black-owned enterprises. They believed that black economic power could lead to political power, a reduction in racism, and greater black trust in and respect for their own group.

In spite of all the obstacles, blacks made an effort to access the economic structure. Numerous black-owned businesses sprang up in the South after the Civil War, many growing out of the mutual aid and fraternal orders the freedmen created to help themselves. They included banks, grocery stores, restaurants, funeral homes, barber and beauty shops, newspapers, and other services needed in the segregated South. By the 1920s, Arthur G. Gaston Sr. had a small conglomerate of such services in Alabama. Nonetheless, black business success was limited, and political power was nonexistent in the areas where most blacks lived.

The fortunes of blacks first began to improve when limits were placed on European immigration during World War I. The opportunities for industrial jobs that followed set off a northward migration that would have both positive and troublesome effects. Two million moved North in the three decades after 1910, three million more in the 1940s. And many moved from the rural South to Southern cities. Whites were employed first and got the best jobs, but Northern steel mill labor paid better than agricultural labor. My father took a job in the steel mills of East Chicago in 1916 to save the family farm in Alabama after the boll weevil destroyed their cotton crop. Like many, he planned to return south but didn't.

Better black jobs benefited black business. Through hard work and determination some black businesses thrived even at the regional and national levels. The legendary Madam C. J. Walker became the first black woman millionaire in the early 1900s by creating hair products and selling them door-to-door at first, then regionally and nationally. S. B. Fuller did the same with cosmetics and household products. Several insurance companies achieved significant size, reach, and influence by the mid–twentieth century; the largest was Supreme Life in Chicago.

In his book *Succeeding Against the Odds,* John H. Johnson, one of the nation's most impressive entrepreneurs, tells his own success story. Johnson describes the way he was identified as someone with potential, given a job and an opportunity to interact with and learn from Harry Herbert Pace, the African-American head of Supreme Life. Johnson also learned much from the company's network of people involved in political, economic, and social activities related to company interests. In 1942 he began to use his knowledge and contacts to establish what eventually became the highly successful Johnson Publishing Company (publishers of *Ebony* and *Jet* magazines) and other enterprises.

In the few situations in which violence and other forms of resistance didn't prevail, black business success, even before Johnson and others, at mid-twentieth century, looked a lot like white business success. In West Virginia, a Southern state that remained with the Union, C. H. James & Son's, a produce commission house, was established in Charlotte in 1883. It is the oldest continuous black business. Its current head, C. H. James III, has moved the company into food processing and has expanded it through acquisitions.

In a 1920 interview the company's founder explained that he got started by selling trinkets from backpacks. Farmers paid in produce, which he and his brothers then sold in town. His competitors ignored him at first, which caused him to work even harder. When they felt his presence, they asked him to join their association to establish "a common understanding and to protect our mutual interest." He later became an executive officer of the association and a member of the Chamber of Commerce. The local bank and other businesses extended him full courtesies. He hired and inspired black office and production workers. But James's experience was a rare exception.

Black business very often experienced severely limiting discrimination and violence. When S. B. Fuller moved toward a major market share in the cosmetics business, reports began to circulate about his racial identity. After his white salespeople from the South attended a meeting and discovered their boss was black, they quit.

In *Black Wallstreet*, Ron Wallace and Jay J. Wilson describe how on June 1, 1921, the black business district of Tulsa, Oklahoma, burned to the ground. The Ku Klux Klan, working with ranking city officials and sympathizers, was believed to be responsible. The estimates of black deaths ranged from three hundred to three thousand. This event of course had a chilling effect on black economic activity everywhere.

Without political and economic power, and reasonable protection by the law, significant connections to the mainstream economy could not take place. Blacks were denied the benefits of network or apprentice education created through participation in government, private corporations, and association with rich individuals. Blacks were an excluded caste group, subject to all manner of attack, and the resultant psychological and social damage.

■ The New Opportunity Structure

Harry Truman's decision to integrate the armed forces in 1948 was probably influenced by the remarkable performance of the Tuskegee Airmen in World War II, although their feats were not told to the general public. Jackie Robinson's entry into white-only major league baseball in 1947, and his outstanding performance under pressure, also had a powerful positive effect. The quiet successes by black individuals in families and at school, work, and play weakened the arguments that undergirded segregation, setting the stage for the Supreme Court decision that outlawed school segregation in 1954. And by this time the black community had a sufficiently large and well-educated leadership group to make the case.

Despite its difficult history, the black community entered the 1950s probably one generation away from greatly reducing its vulnerability. According to Jaynes and Williams in *A Common Destiny*, "until the 1960s, 75 percent of black households with a child under the age of eighteen included both husband and wife." The desire for education was high. There were jobs for blacks in such professions as teaching, social work, and manufacturing. Black communities were reasonably safe.

The 1954 Supreme Court decision in *Brown v. Board of Education* ended legal school segregation. Kenneth B. Clark, a black psychologist, gave important and telling testimony showing the psychological damage segregation does to black children. The decision was important because it broke the most powerful symbol of black inferiority and raised the question of why blacks were being excluded in public accommodations, or anywhere. But school segregation was only one source of the psychological damage being done to blacks.

More potent damage resulted from the past and present exclusion of black families from full participation in the mainstream economy. Reasonably well-paying jobs demanding little education had lifted the immigrant masses, but such jobs were not open to blacks. It is ironic that the end of legal discrimination in public accommodations served to further weaken an already weak black business community. For while blacks were largely closed out of doing business beyond the black community, the black consumer could shop anywhere he wished.

The cracks in the caste system led to the intensification in the 1960s of the black civil rights movement. A vibrant and determined people, with its church-based call for equal rights, improved racial attitudes on the part of whites, and a new technology—television—gave the movement significant power. Vivid television scenes of a Southern governor blocking the doors of the state university to his black constituents, police and their dogs attacking black citizens, and black school children being jeered by white mobs—clearly unacceptable conduct in a democracy—added strong fuel.

The black church culture was a spiritual, social, mind-setting, direction-giving vehicle. But it was not connected to the mainstream economic system. If my father had not been able to earn a living, how long could my family have sustained the values of the church in a society based on economic achievement? It was the fact that he could earn just enough from the steel mill to give us the basic things we needed—the food, clothes, and shelter that enabled us to feel adequate—that allowed us to sustain a sense of dignity, purpose, and value.

It quickly became apparent that the political power gained in the 1960s could only be greatly effective in promoting group interests when working in tandem with economic power. There was a resurgence of a need for the kind of economic power that ownership creates.

Black Enterprise magazine, founded in 1970 by Earl G. Graves, a seminal business and civic leader himself, chronicles the reemergence of significant black businesses. *BE* noted that two of the twenty-five most significant events in shaping modern black business development were the Small Business Administration set-aside program for minority business in 1968, and President Nixon's 1969 signing of Executive Order 11458 that led to the establishment of the Minority Business Development Agency. These two programs represent the nation's first efforts to compensate for past exclusion from economic opportunities and to counteract its harmful effects, particularly the absence of a black economic leadership group.

What is important here is that in 1970, unlike 1870, blacks could vote and had become a part, albeit small, of the larger political and economic structures. The political and economic system that others had used to build community was beginning to work a little bit for blacks, more than a hundred years late.

African-American congressman Parren J. Mitchell attached set-aside requirements to many government spending programs throughout the 1970s and 1980s. In consequence the number of black-owned firms rose from 187,602 with receipts of about $5.6 billion in 1972 to 424,165 with receipts of more than $20 billion in 1987. This was a 126 percent increase in firms and a 257 percent increase in receipts. But these impressive gains brought blacks to only 2.4 percent ownership of all businesses with 0.19 percent of total receipts. Unfortunately, the improved attitudes and conditions came woefully late, and the policies and programs of the 1950s and 1960s addressed only a part of the problem.

Despite impressive growth, the black business segment is not even close to being large enough to provide many job and career opportunities. And not enough black mainstream economic leaders exist to serve as role models and mentors who connect the young to the networks that lead to mainstream economic and social success.

■ Rapid Change: The Best of Times, and the Worst of Times

With the onset of the postindustrial age, mainstream groups had the best chance of meeting the demands of the new economy. Black gains had come so late that taking advantage of the new opportunities appeared to require an individual effort not connected to the community.

An African-American blue-collar worker who was active in the civil rights movement of the 1960s lamented that his son, a state trooper, feels he has no special responsibility to the black community, because he got his job by passing qualifying tests. Before the 1960s a passing score still wouldn't have gotten him the job. But with all it accomplished, the civil rights movement was just that, a movement, and not a systematic cohesion-building effort grounded in cooperative problem-solving institutions—one problem being the transmission of knowledge and skills to the next generation.

A bifurcation began to develop in the black community. Those with adequate education, support, or mainstream ties were enjoying more access than ever before. Yet even with support the challenge is great. Recall that I needed my university instructor and my social network to reassure me that I was able and had a right to be in the state college. The problem still exists. The white-power-black-exclusion message in the weight of history is great, complicating the identification with mainstream people and institutions that is needed to function adequately in them.

Whites from poor backgrounds report similar initial feelings. But they blend in better; identifying comes easier. They are not harassed because of their race. Any number of examples come to mind. A white man being admitted to a psychiatric ward on the West Coast promised the assembled doctors that he would do well as long as they did not let "that nigger" put his hands on him. He was referring to the sole black psychiatrist present. Nobody took exception to the slur; no one supported their colleague. When challenged later, the doctor in charge said it was not his responsibility. Interestingly, the offending patient later apologized because his fellow mental patients told him that his behavior was unacceptable.

In the 1960s, many African-American young people without adequate family and social network support, mainstream skills, and attendant confidence were unable to enter a mainstream economy that was becoming increasingly complex. The difficulty was compounded by the tendency of employers to use education level as an indicator of personal discipline and reliability, even when the job did not require a high level of education.

A further problem is that in the past black people who achieved economic success remained in their neighborhoods, but for the last generation or so, some black children have been growing up in the mainstream, with few if any ties to the old neighborhoods and low-income friends their parents and grandparents had. The natural connections, understanding, and rapport between these two groups is now missing.

Suburbanization and the decline of well-paying low-skill jobs has led to concentrated poverty. Too many black children are growing up without successful role models and mentors around them. And the larger social conditions that have led to a decline in the influence of religion have affected the black church as well, intensifying community and family deterioration. These two lacks make the task of promoting wider mainstream participation that much more complex.

These are the conditions that some call self-inflicted, that are blamed on limited ability and effort. The history just outlined is not generally taught to the citizens of our democracy, not even to those with the responsibility for making policy and program decisions. Believing the myths that intelligence determines outcome and that the playing field is level, good people can hear about a desperately depressed young woman and her children in a roach-infested house (the ones we met in chapter 2) and argue that it is entirely her fault.

The overall pattern of success within the community suggests the validity of my argument, as well as what can be done. Consider that in many highly selective university programs half or more of the black students are of Caribbean backgrounds; among nonimmigrant blacks, the students are the children of church leaders, now often a generation removed; and women significantly outnumber men.

While many factors contribute to this, the most important are (1) ability to reject the negative identities imposed by the larger society, (2) a group-based source of effective attitudes, values, and behaviors, and (3) less resistance from the larger society. (In the case of women, because many of them were domestic workers, they posed less of a threat to power; also, they have recently been beneficiaries of the women's movement.)

Let us now go on to discuss how such conditions can be created to overcome the negative effects of the past and to promote participation and belonging for many more African-Americans.

PART THREE:

WIN-WIN

CHAPTER
6

PARTICIPATION AND BELONGING

As the twenty-first century approaches, the effects of the global economy are being felt. Wage stagnation, downsizing, outsourcing, and other adjustments to cut the cost of doing business are threatening the security of all American workers. In tandem, the traditional American response to economic and social insecurity has intensified—scapegoating.

The current wave of scapegoating threatens not only its black targets but the entire nation, for it prevents all Americans from addressing the real challenge of the present and future: how to strengthen families and communities even as the global economy steadily reduces the connection of many households to living-wage jobs.

Opportunistic politicians have convinced much of the public that the problems of our day have been caused by self-inflicted family deterioration: out-of-wedlock childbirth, welfare dependency, and crime due to moral decay. Many associate these and other bad behaviors with vulnerable minority groups.

With blacks as the designated scapegoats, young people in particular are bombarded by negative images harmful to their development. The black community has no systematic way to counter these and transmit the positive. Without the strong church-based communities that once performed the function naturally, many young people are traumatized, they underperform, or act out in troublesome ways, and become part of the "evidence" used to scapegoat.

Before the nation can create a win-win mentality, it will be necessary to decrease vulnerability of all groups to scapegoating and increase their participation and sense of belonging—conditions that encourage desirable behavior. Members of minority groups in particular need to assume leadership roles, but they must also collaborate with leaders of the larger society in a process fair and beneficial to the entire society.

Participation and belonging are the right of all U.S. citizens and legal immigrants. But in this chapter I draw on black community experience for two reasons: because blacks are the "designated problem group" and because it is the experience I am most familiar with. The approaches I discuss, though, are applicable to all vulnerable groups.

As legal segregation ended in the 1950s and 1960s, blacks and whites expected American institutions to work for blacks as they had for others in the past. But as I described in the previous chapter, blacks faced exceptional obstacles. In addition, the already established political and economic structures did not suddenly accept young black people into the mainstream. While legal segregation was being dismantled, resistance in the larger society remained.

Several years ago an African-American board member of a large bank encountered a black teller who was angry because, as in years past, all of the summer employees were white students. The board member spoke with the chief executive officer, a white man who had a strong commitment to minority employment. After an investigation revealed a pattern of discrimination, the personnel officer involved was reassigned and black students were employed. But there are not enough black board members and others with significant influence in mainstream economic institutions.

Much black community energy was consumed in the effort to open up all aspects of the system, especially education. But no systematic effort was made in the black community or larger society to overcome the psychological damage of past exclusion and abuse. The most pervasive has continued to be the general perception and depiction of the group.

Even today the media and some politicians focus predominantly on black problems and not black successes. That allows people to say that there is nothing wrong with the system, there's something wrong with blacks. They are imagined as poor, dependent, criminal, or at best, jazzy or exotic—except for Michael Jordan, Oprah Winfrey, Bill Cosby, Colin Powell, and a few others.

For many, this perception is not overt but only unconscious. For instance, a film producer, in rejecting a story about a successful black family, commented, "What's black about it? That could have been a white story." In another example, the president of a university responded to a recruitment day question from a white parent about diversity by discussing the scholarships they were awarding minorities. A black mother in the audience pointed out that she and her husband, a businessman, had sent four children to Ivy League undergraduate and professional schools without a dime of scholarship money. She obviously felt his answer implied that all blacks are poor, and losers—a view that blacks who have become well off, often through remarkable effort, naturally resent. In a quick recovery, the president cited the mother's family as an additional example of diversity.

Lest one think that affirmative action has changed people's views, remember that my Professor Bobron in the 1950s could not tolerate the idea that a black student could have an A paper. It didn't fit his image of blacks. A very successful young professional black woman, born into three generations of affluence, told me, "It all just makes me tired, sad, and sometimes even depressed."

Even many people who would like to do the right thing would prefer to look forward rather than examine the ill effects of the past. This approach underestimates the complexity of the task. It contributes to the creation of ineffective policies that then convince more people that nothing can be done. Without assigning blame or being judgmental, we must acknowledge and address the full effects of past policies and practices and the magnitude of today's task.

Observations made by economists Jessica Gordon Nembhard and Tanya Lewis in a draft document for the Black Community Crusade for Children, "An Economic Development Report," underscore that

> the status of African-Americans in the U.S. economy is in many ways similar to that of a Third World country on the periphery of the industrialized First World:
>
> 1. High and increasing levels of unemployment
> 2. High and increasing levels of poverty
> 3. Concentration in low level jobs with low earnings and advancement potentials
> 4. Limited small business and entrepreneurial success
> 5. Chronic health problems which interfere with productivity
> 6. A resurgence of discrimination and reduced national commitment to Affirmative Action
>
> In turn these conditions contribute to the growing polarization between the African-American middle and lower classes, the breakdown of family and community life, crime, substance abuse, etc.

■ Self-Help

To those who say that blacks should try to help themselves, the simple answer is: They've been doing that ever since slavery ended—and even before. There has been a long-standing self-help tradition in the African-American community. Recall that almost twenty percent of the money for schools for freedmen came from an impoverished black community. With minimal help the community seeded the fortunes of their own. There were also many self-help societies that formed during slavery and expanded after emancipation. John Hope Franklin, the distinguished African-American historian, points out that self-help was a necessity because help from the outside was very limited.

In the first White House Conference on Children in 1909, black representatives expressed the view that there was no need to develop programs for black orphans because black extended families take care of their own. That was always my experience as well: Dr. Charles Boyd, an African-American, didn't charge our family anything for medical care once it was clear that our parents wanted to send all five of us to college. Also, my mother and I would visit and care for an old woman we knew as Granny, who was not a relative. This was typical of the way much of the community acted.

Contrary to current claims, there is an almost desperate interest in "doing something"—self-help—among African-Americans. When the story of the Children's Defense Fund's Black Community Crusade for Children was shown on Black Entertainment Television, the telephone lines were flooded with people who wanted to help, some in tears. Over the last few years I have met or consulted with numerous African-American individuals and groups that are engaged in some kind of self-help activity. For example, a black woman who had just inherited some property asked my advice about how she might use it to help black families. And every fraternal and social organization I belong to is involved in efforts to encourage young people.

Nonetheless, self-help is not enough. In *A Hand Up: Black Philanthropy and Self-Help in America*, Emmett D. Carson shows that much of the self-help, though significant, is small in scale, informal, and fragmented because the community—

with a few individual exceptions—does not have significant wealth. Opportunities need to be opened up in the wider society.

Resistance in the private sector has led to disproportionate employment of African-Americans in public sector jobs. Dinesh D'Souza, in *The End of Racism*, points to this as a weakness rather than necessary and reasonable. Yet his charge of black overreliance on government ignores that many businesses were and are at this very moment financed and assisted by government.

Quite apart from the land handouts while the country was spreading across the continent, the fact is that business has become progressively more socialized. The government has spent billions on "set-asides" to agribusiness corporations to keep certain products out of production. The research and development that led to our modern communications industry was paid for largely by the government and turned over to the private sector. And the Carnegie Commission on Science, Technology, and Government in September 1992 reported, "In the early 1980s, several industrial states, suffering a deep and intractable manufacturing recession, formed new partnerships with industry and academic researchers, aimed at building economic strength through the development and deployment of technology." Across the country, states began sharing research costs.

In a *Time* magazine article (March 25, 1996) Karen Tumulty wrote: "By some estimates, the government funnels up to $75 billion a year to business, enough to account for almost half the federal deficit. The Agriculture Department, for instance, will spend $110 million this year to advertise overseas everything from V8 juice to Friskies." Product promotion subsidies from government in 1995, to name but two, were $1.1 million and $2.6 million to Campbell Soup and E & J Gallo Winery respectively.

So, clearly the government assists in creating opportunities for many, in helping people make it. But this same government is then criticized for the "peanuts" for commu-

nity and economic development that would create an opportunity structure in black communities. Yet programs that
strengthen black participation in the economic mainstream
are our only chance to address social problems in a humane way.

Republican vice-presidential candidate Jack Kemp and
Democratic senator Joe Lieberman have pointed out that
the nation can't just build a fence around inner-city communities and walk away. Big-city mayors from both parties, such
as Republican Brett Shindler of Jersey City and Democrat
Kurt Schmoke of Baltimore, are giving significant attention
to bringing community-building economic activity back to
these cities.

The Democratic Leadership Committee, Empower America, and the Progressive Policy Institute are all looking at tax
code changes that will bring economic activity to inner cities.
They all realize that you can't reduce illegitimate economic
activity without restoring legitimate economic activity.

I don't want to minimize the problems in areas that have
lost their economic lifeblood. Restoring the circulation and
wider distribution of legal money in them—and a related
sense of community and order—will be difficult. And it
cannot be done in a "trickle-down" way. In short, in difficult
times an effort must be made to create a rising economic
tide that can lift boats that have been tied to the bottom or
caught in tangled ropes and ancient wrecks.

■ Toward Greater African-American Access

The first phase of access involves breaking the black caste
status. The second is protecting and preparing the group,
particularly the young, for participation and belonging in
the mainstream economy and community through an approach that addresses mainstream needs.

Many black groups are still locked in the first-phase protest mode needed for the struggle to secure human and civil rights. In the first phase the issue and the enemy were clear. The issue was the abuse permitted and promoted by legal segregation and custom, and the enemy was everyone who supported the system. The abuse was "in your face" on a daily basis, and the urgency was ever present. This created a common cause. The strategy was straightforward—legal action and high-visibility protest.

As a result of being locked in the first-phase protest mode, there is no need for ongoing analysis, planning, and coordinated action in the second phase, despite the fact that traditional institutions, in the black community or the larger society, are not bringing about desired outcomes. Existing efforts are fragmented and episodic, providing no systematic way to build cohesion and help the young avail themselves of opportunity within the mainstream.

What I will propose here may seem like a long, slow, frustrating process for those who need immediate solutions. But there is no quick fix. At best it will take twenty to thirty years. Flashes of power and hope can be prompted through exhortation and demonstration, but these flashes cannot be sustained. Frustration can deepen into demoralization. The magnitude of the problem, the historical tensions and distrust, and the cycles of hope and despair can destroy organizations and efforts despite the best of intentions.

The approach needed is a simultaneous and coordinated focus on African-American economic, community, and youth development. This approach can overcome the negative effects of the past, promote self- and group appreciation, increase cohesion and power, and position young people to participate as full members in the mainstream society.

In a *Harvard Business Review* article, Michael E. Porter discussed the entrepreneurial potential of the inner cities, listing the following possible pluses: strategic location, unmet local market needs, collections or clusters of related companies, and, despite the myth, willing and able workers.

"Inner-city businesses," he wrote, "should be profitable, and positioned not only to serve the local community but also to export to the surrounding economy." The article noted, however, that community leaders too often drive businesses out of town by expecting them also to meet social needs. Other negative factors included antibusiness attitudes, limited employee and management skills, and security problems. These problems, it seems to me, largely coincide with unmet youth needs.

Youths respond to opportunity. A group of black teens in Los Angeles planned to "have some fun," scaring the white people who had been attracted to a festival in a local park. The police began to mobilize to control and protect. A local black entrepreneur, the actress Marla Gibbs, arrived and reminded the young people that she was able to provide them with jobs in her restaurant and in other local places because outsiders were not afraid to come into the neighborhood. The teens then thought better of their plan and left.

That exchange was fortuitous. And I agree that business can't meet all the social needs of a community. But it can train and employ young people, and many businesses can benefit from collaboration with organizations involved in youth development. Businesses and youth organizations in a sustained relationship could provide direction and an ongoing support network for young people, could help them develop constructive goals and the skills to meet them. And there is no question that such a positive program would be good for businesses in areas under economic and social stress.

But a larger African-American leadership presence in community and economic development is needed. And the leadership must be committed to promoting improved group conditions as much as personal gains. Many African-Americans have a special concern and knowledge about their own people, and because of this, they have a special determination and endurance. This is crucial. It is difficult for disadvantaged people to identify with community and economic development goals without a fellow African-American presence.

Unfortunately, the long-standing problems of limited access to capital, inexperience, and lack of a network hold down the number of black economic leaders. No single segment of the society—business, government, nonprofit service organizations, or the black community—can by itself adequately address these several needs. But they can be met through coordinated, cooperative efforts.

While all sectors must play a role, and the community, economic, and youth focus must be simultaneous, a youth focus linked to black community organizations is key. Power grown from meaningful, effective community effort to serve the young can be sustained.

A focus on youth also makes tactical sense. Sustained deep involvement with young people can create the sense of urgency that is needed in and outside the black community. It is a way to overcome the inertia caused by the past focus on civil rights. The youth cause can mobilize resources across the spectrum of African-Americans. It can provide an opportunity to limit fracturing of the African-American community. Addressing the needs of young people can suggest a community agenda for the division of labor, the organization, and the activities needed to promote cohesion and participation. And a black community focus on youth will help in enlisting support from the larger society.

Most Americans still believe that it is important to prepare children to become responsible citizens and workers. The strategy of those who believe that blacks and other minorities are not worthy has been to suppress investment in these groups and to develop "scientific evidence" to buttress their position. Since the naysayers are much more vocal, programs like Head Start, though difficult to destroy, are difficult to support at the necessary level. Yet it should be remembered that "not able" was the argument about the European immigrant masses that Congressman Justin

Smith Morrill had to contend with when developing the federal land-grant college programs in the 1860s—and many of today's political and business leaders are the happy result of that investment. Indeed, even many of those opposed to social investment programs today were themselves the beneficiaries of such programs—the postwar G.I. Bill, for example.

Youth efforts should, from the outset, enlist the young people themselves. Organization-based, ethical, and responsible activity on their own behalf and on behalf of the community can provide a powerful sense of purpose and direction. In the process, the value of consistent personal excellence and good citizenship conduct can be learned.

Perhaps as important, the many successes of blacks will continue to be considered unusual—the efforts of individuals—until there is highly visible, effective community action and wider success among black youth. And the black community itself has to highlight its successes. For example, this past year the national chess championship for middle school students was won by black youngsters from Harlem. It was not immediately or widely reported in the New York media. Very able black youth will continue to be limited by the messages from the larger society and by their own related performance until the "designated loser" label is systematically attacked and laid to rest.

There are many youth-centered programs in the community. Below, I discuss several familiar to me. These programs provide insights and suggest directions. They show the wide span of interest and concern, and they represent different resource pools that can be greatly expanded as well as knitted together. And they involve young people with the greatest need.

The projects I discuss developed independently of each other. Yet they have common and instructive threads: They enable young people to make strong attachments to caring, positive mentors and guides in safe, meaningful institutions. They bring generations together, and some encourage peers to help one another. They help young people to establish goals as well as the competence, confidence, and guidance needed to achieve them. They make possible a positive racial and personal identity at a time of life when negative messages in the greater society can be most harmful to black children. They bring different segments of the black community together and, in some cases, the black and larger communities. They impart to youth an appreciation of their responsibilities to themselves, their group, and our society.

All of this will be needed to prepare more young people to be at home in the economic mainstream.

■ "Leave No Child Behind"

In 1990 Marian Wright Edelman, founder and president of the Children's Defense Fund, pulled together a group of African-Americans interested in helping black youth: political activists, religious leaders, social and youth service personnel, representatives of advocacy organizations, academics, college students, and professional people. The Black Community Crusade for Children (BCCC) emerged from this effort after several years of planning to forge a broad base of support.

With the rallying theme of "Leave No Child Behind," the BCCC mission is to ensure that every child has a Healthy Start, a Head Start, a Fair Start, a Safe Start, and a Moral Start in life. It identifies strategies for reestablishing the bonds of community that can make these outcomes possible for children. The BCCC then helps people in local communities to employ these strategies.

The BCCC provides information, technical assistance, and a support network for neighborhood-based leaders. Many such leaders, and people in areas related to the five Starts— juvenile and family court judges, teachers, parents, faith community members, college students—receive training at the former Alex Haley farm. Doing such work in this place, where the author of *Roots* lived, has great symbolic meaning. The local leaders enlist their communities in carrying out projects designed to achieve the five Starts.

Several BCCC activities—house parties, Freedom Schools, Black Student Leadership Network (BSLN)—are of great interest to me. They are models for addressing needs I have discussed: black community cohesion and effective action that elicits mainstream support for black youth development and participation.

On a nationwide annual day—the date the farm was established—celebrities in entertainment and sports, professional and business people, folk from all walks of life, each sponsor a house party to raise funds for BCCC (matched by a contribution from a national foundation, the Charles Stewart Mott). The party serves to introduce the work and goals of BCCC and to mobilize many segments of communities in support of black children. Again, there is cultural resonance. Blacks working at the margins of the economy once combined socializing and making ends meet by holding rent parties.

The Freedom Schools are one of the BCCC activities that benefit from house parties and address each of the five Start missions. These are local summer programs for elementary-age students that provide knowledge and appreciation of black culture, academic and social skills, particularly conflict resolution aimed at reducing violence, and a first taste of participation in service activities. Eventually these programs will be held year-round after school or on weekends. Parents are engaged in promoting the development of their children. A variety of local organizations and people are involved in supporting these programs, providing space, money, and tutors. In 1996 there were twenty-seven Freedom School sites in fifteen cities, and more than five thousand students have been involved since its inception.

A key feature is the involvement of black college students through BSLN. More than six hundred have been trained at

Haley. They serve as teachers and tutors and, through their training, they connect with leaders of the civil rights movement from the generation before. Thus there is a three-generation connection and message transmission. And while service and social action is a part of the message, the central message is about personal development and responsibility to self, the group, and the society.

Dwayne Crompton, who directs the very successful Kansas City BCCC program and Freedom Schools, points out that the churches, the college students, community leaders, parents, and students all benefit. Enthusiasm, direction, mutual support and renewal, college scholarships, and other benefits have grown from coming together to help children.

■ St. HOPE Academy

Kevin Johnson, a National Basketball Association all-star and a member of Dream Team II, founded St. HOPE Academy in 1989 in the neighborhood where he grew up, Oak Park, just south of Sacramento, California. HOPE stands for Help Our People Excel. A saint, according to the youth organization's creed, is someone who helps others.

Oak Park is a depressed neighborhood where the median income of $14,732 is less than half that in Sacramento. Many of the program's participants are influenced by gang and drug culture, lack positive role models and guidance, and come from dysfunctional families. The academy provides them with opportunities for educational, cultural, spiritual, and social experiences and expression. The forty-eight children aged eight to thirteen in the program come for one and a half hours each day of the school year and all day long during the summer for individual tutoring, meals, workshops, club activities, and special programs. Students in an older group aged fourteen to eighteen receive school guidance, SAT preparation, counseling, and employment placement. These "graduates" also tutor the younger children.

St. HOPE has a creed of honesty, fair play, hard work, and healthy living; it teaches an honor code; and it is committed to inculcating faith, hope, and charity. This orientation raises students' self-esteem and the expectation of achieving the academy's five objectives: scholastic improvement, citizenship improvement, reduction in truancy, improvement in high school graduation rates, and increasing college attendance and employment rates. The academy offers programs to develop and build character through community service work, African-American history lessons, Scripture memorization, and physical fitness. Students' parents become engaged in academy life. Students are paired with community-based mentors. Four times a year the academy's FEASTs (Friends Eating and Sharing Together) with volunteer families give the students an opportunity to observe how other families interact in their homes and around their dinner tables. Its WEB program (Wise Elderly Bunch) invites elders in the community to share their life experiences. The Neighborhood Improvement Team gives the students hands-on experience in community improvement and service to the needy and elderly.

Supported in its fund-raising by California Governor and Mrs. Pete Wilson and Kevin Johnson's Phoenix Suns teammates, the academy now has trained two hundred active volunteers.

▪ Project SPIRIT

Started in 1986 and sponsored by the National Council of Black Churches, Project SPIRIT is a third important prototype. With the support of caring parents, pastors, and teachers there are now sixty-five SPIRIT program sites around the country. The project is designed to foster in children aged six through twelve the personal qualities and values needed to be a successful adult, partner, parent, worker, and citizen. The six qualities that give the program its name are Strength, Perseverance, Imagination, Responsibility, Integrity, and Talent. Program goals are:

- To increase children's awareness of themselves and their culture and to enhance their self-esteem
- To improve the children's school performance and their appreciation of math and science
- To inspire parents to be more loving through more effective nurturing, guidance, and supervision practices
- To enhance pastors' capacity to assess and counsel their congregations on current family and community issues
- To facilitate meaningful involvement of community members in supporting children and families

Some aspects of the program are specific to African-American children. Other aspects, like the educational support in math and science, communications and media arts, and economic resource development and distribution programs are being used by children from other backgrounds as well.

Funded by the operating budgets of churches, the program's hard-working volunteers are congregation members and active and retired public school teachers. So many children have expressed a desire to continue that Project SPIRIT is now planning a program for adolescents.

■ Westchester Clubmen

The Clubmen, operating in Westchester County, New York, is a civic and social organization of African-American physicians, educators, attorneys, senior corporate and foundation officers, and people in the arts—Gordon Parks and the late Cab Calloway, for example. The Clubmen have sponsored many programs for minority children and adolescents. At three sites, licensed teachers and aides were paid to provide intensive tutoring in verbal and math skills needed for the PSAT and SAT tests, assisted by Clubmen and members of the 369th Veterans' Association. Dozens of minority youths have entered colleges and qualified for scholarships as a result of this program. The Clubmen's Foundation once awarded students $2,500 per year for four years of undergraduate study.

The organization provides at-risk preadolescent and adolescent African-American males with the concerted support they need to complete high school and successfully embark on higher education, including personal and career counseling. After-school activities include tutoring, social skills training, organized sports, discussions, chess, computer classes, creative writing, and field trips.

The Clubmen also support the young men's parents, helping single mothers, joining them in meetings at school, and providing advice on how to deal with the youngsters' occasional problems. For example, one Clubmen member, a lawyer, helped a family avert a threatened eviction.

Hugh Price, my colleague and a member of Clubmen, said, "It is not possible to know the impact of a program which is so new and too modest in scale to be subjected to scientific evaluation. Nevertheless, we do have some encouraging preliminary feedback." School staff members are enthusiastic and report seeing improvements in the quantity and quality of work performed by the young people. The boys are said to be more cooperative and active in class and less likely to engage in disruptive behavior. The program has helped with the youngsters' social development as well. Clubmen who have taken small groups on special outings (to restaurants, to Rockefeller Center, on tours) have been struck by the young people's newly found social polish and ease of interaction.

■ The National Academy Foundation

The National Academy Foundation is an important model of local, national, public, and private sector cooperation to create a diversified work force and to enable the benefits of work and economic activity to penetrate all areas of the society. It lays a needed emphasis on economic integration more than school racial integration, on inclusion in place of exclusion, with important psychological and social benefits for students and employers, minority and majority community members alike. *It is not charity: There are mutual business and social benefits.*

The Foundation was established in 1982 by Sandy Weill, then chief executive officer of the American Express Corporation. Vernon Jordan, the prominent African-American attorney, civil rights leader, and presidential adviser, was chairman of the board for seven years.

The travel industry needed qualified workers from diverse backgrounds. This led to the creation of an Academy of Finance, an Academy of Travel and Tourism, and an Academy of Public Service, operating as curriculum and instructional programs within high schools serving minority students. A number of businesses provide summer internships for them.

The students' participation in work outside school often informs and enriches, and sometimes even changes, the school's program. NAF has helped many teenagers organize their lives for school and future success. NAF did not target the top and already college-bound students. Many of its students, able but not directing themselves, were underachieving. They were not (or thought they were not) receiving the positive feedback from school that they needed. Goal-directed, structured activities improved the students' performance and secured the feedback.

In college, many of them do not go into the specific program areas taught by the academy. But the NAF project exposure enables the students to sense career possibilities. It is from such work that many will identify entrepreneurial potentials in the mainstream, in inner cities, and in their respective ethnic communities.

■ Economic Activity in Youth and Community Development

Economist Edward Irons points out that even when economic activity produces only a few jobs, it is still a positive force in poor communities where businesses, jobs, and income hardly exist. The psychological and social benefits are important. Again, economic activity can give direction and purpose to young people, schools, businesses, and community as with the NAF programs mentioned above.

The African-American community cannot afford to be without an economic thrust, which should build on economic activity already in place. But as discussed, many stressed communities have little of such activity or of the network of business and service people and relationships needed to support it. Current strategies such as Empowerment Zones, Enterprise Communities, the Community Reinvestment Act, and a growing number of community development banks—public, private, and nonprofit groups— are designed to address this business infrastructure problem.

Empowerment Zones are to involve community-based public, private, nonprofit, religious, education, and other groups in an effort to attract private investment, economic activity, and jobs. In short, tax incentives, capital sources, and coordinated human services are being systematically put together in the same way such forces come together in less stressed communities, and in turn create jobs, pride, and desirable community and family functioning.

Some of these programs have school and parental involvement programs. But there is still a "bricks and mortar" or housing emphasis in community development and a too narrow profit motive in business initiatives. All of these activities can be more effective through a greater youth and people development focus. And in the black community these efforts must simultaneously create cohesion and power that can promote participation and belonging within the larger society. Let us first consider two helpful models.

■ The Marshall Heights Community Development Organization

The work of Lloyd Smith and the Marshall Heights Community Development Organization (MHCDO) in northeast Washington, D.C., is a very important model. They have taken a holistic approach rather than one focused on bricks and mortar and making money. The MHCDO has a partnership with Richardson Elementary School, which is implementing our Yale School Development Program. Business, housing, and human services are put together in a way to facilitate economic and family functioning in this almost entirely black community.

The organization began when a few residents got together to address issues such as inadequate streets and sidewalks, storm drainage, and decaying housing. Two years later it was incorporated in order to work with the District of Columbia's Department of Housing and Community Development. In 1980, as an outgrowth of a conference that targeted economics and business development as the way to renew the community, it became the Marshall Heights Community Development Organization.

It has a fifty-nine-member board of directors; twenty-three citizens-at-large and representatives of three churches, three businesses, nine public housing associations, and twenty-one civic associations and neighborhood and commercial area groups. The board meets ten times a year. The directors and staff initiate and supervise projects, but the board is committed to avoiding micromanagement. This permits community involvement and effective professional management. About half of the management team are community residents, and half are outside development experts with experience in other neighborhoods.

When I visited MHCDO, several members of the staff were busy preparing for an art show and sale, "Creative Visions, East of the River," sponsored jointly with the Ward Seven Arts Consortium and Friends. The area is on the less glamorous but once reasonably prosperous side of the Anacostia River, which divides the city. Beautiful paintings by mostly local African-American artists were being prepared for display. A large and appreciative group attended the exhibition.

A mural depicting black achievers, stretching the full length of a building, borders the $10-million shopping center that is the centerpiece of MHCDO programs. The organization has a forty-percent equity in the fully occupied center, and the businesses in it are making money. Among them are a national chain supermarket, a national chain pharmacy, a bank, a laundry, a flower shop, a barber and beauty shop, a clothing store, and a much prized bagel restaurant. The owner of the bagel restaurant is black and was formerly a McDonald's restaurant manager. His is one of five black-owned businesses of the eighteen currently in the complex.

When a few residents groused about the presence of a Korean merchant, a black businessman reminded them that they no longer had to travel long distances for services because people like the Korean merchant felt comfortable enough to invest in the community. The Korean merchant, though, did take the businessman's advice and hired black workers.

The MHCDO is working to promote entrepreneurial skills and activities among young black people. By selecting stores to meet resident needs, it increased discretionary spending inside the community from 20 percent to 50 percent. At the same time it deliberately avoided liquor stores and other high-profit businesses that would contribute to loitering and other undesirable behavior.

MHCDO has a business incubator, providing services such as loan packaging and marketing assistance, shared expenses for items such as clerical services, maintenance, delivery, and an in-house revolving fund for short-term loans. It has also purchased an area with immediate access to a highway for development as an industrial park.

In a traditional community-development activity—housing—MHCDO has also participated significantly, providing it in a way designed to change the tone of the area. MHCDO built new single-family homes in an area that was once nicknamed Dodge City because of the level of crime and violence. It has worked with the local police to establish a community crime patrol and to move drug activity out of the area. It has built attractive town houses across from the Metro station in order to attract white-collar workers who want to take advantage of the bargains. It has made home ownership possible for families with incomes as low as $11,000 per year, operating on the notion that ownership gives residents a stake in their neighborhood.

MHCDO has participated in the affordable-housing Home Sight program with Fannie Mae, the D.C. government, and private mortgage lenders, purchasing vacant houses, rehabilitating them, and reselling them to low-income buyers. So far, more than a hundred affordable housing units have been made available.

The MHCDO single-resident-occupancy building represents a combination of housing and human service: supportive housing. It would have been called a rooming house previously, but is designed to meet the needs of our time. It is an attractive building with single rooms, a common kitchen, and sitting rooms on every floor. People with physical challenges live in an easy-access area. Others receive counseling and other support right in the building. Here, as in housing throughout the area, the residents are carefully screened. The pride and attention to business of the security guard, counselors, and administrators are common attributes of people in well-run organizations.

There is a transitional housing program for homeless families, with supportive social services to assist them in becoming self-sufficient. MHCDO has a lease/purchase option for qualified families to assume the mortgage and thus own their home upon completing the program. There is also an adoptive-family component for religious and other community groups to provide support and financial assistance to families in the transitional housing program.

MHCDO views human services as front-end investments. The goal is to prevent lifelong problems and promote self-sufficiency so that society won't have to spend as much on jails, welfare dependency, drug treatment, and containment.

MHCDO also has post-secondary education counseling and a GED (general education diploma) coordination program. Other human development projects include job counseling and placement services, life skills training, crisis intervention services, family and child programs, senior citizen services, substance abuse and crime prevention programs, drug treatment and aftercare programs.

These programs are supported by federal, city, and foundation grants, by private fund-raising initiatives, and now by profits from MHCDO's forty percent interest in the shopping center. But given the level of need, this income is not enough. The cost for overhead available through the grants is about four percent, but the actual cost is twenty-two percent. Much of the organization's time goes into fund-raisers such as bake sales and other activities needed to keep and carry out their human service programs.

Lloyd Smith, executive director of MHCDO, is the unquestioned key to the success of this project. He was with the federal and district government in a variety of roles for twenty-seven years before coming to MHCDO in 1980. Under his leadership the staff has risen from four to sixty-four and the annual budget from $115,000 to more than $5.1 million.

The purchase of the shopping center shows Smith's tenacity and vision. His board thought it impossible but nevertheless sanctioned the effort. They accepted a $25,000 venture-capital grant from the Department of Housing and Community Development. After persistent but unsuccessful efforts to find investors, they got the current shopping center's owner to put up a half million dollars, and they got DHCD to put up another three quarters of a million dollars. Along the way Mr. Smith put up his own home as collateral. Two years later, DHCD refinanced the project. The center was appraised at $10 million in 1994, up 67 percent from its 1983 value. New investors included D.C. National Bank, Berman Properties, a Ford Foundation subsidiary, and DHCD.

One of the new investors indicated that his company did not ordinarily do business with community development corporations because their boards are often contentious. This is not uncommon when people who ordinarily have little power gain some in a single area. The private business group participated in this project because the board was cohesive, the staff was very businesslike, and it was good business for their company. There are still many problems in the Marshall Heights area, but the community has made enough progress to know that the decline can be reversed.

■ STEP-UP

There are successful projects similar to Marshall Heights across the country. In some cases the initiative has been taken by local political leadership. In Baltimore, under the direction of Mayor Kurt Schmoke, Daniel P. Henson III combined the renovation of housing with human resource development and employment in a project called STEP-UP, embodying the hope that economic activity will combat some of the problems of crime, drugs, and poverty that are due to a lack of jobs. In November 1995, I visited Baltimore to learn more about the mayor's initiatives in the last three to four years.

The STEP-UP project is designed to empower some of the eighteen thousand residents of public housing in Baltimore. Nearly half of the households in the area are made up of a single parent and children. The average net income is $6,094, and two-thirds receive some form of public assistance. At the heart of the approach is a year-long onsite apprenticeship program in which residents work side by side with skilled union craftsmen in the construction trades. They rotate among different trades throughout the period. They receive practical instructions and job-readiness skills, math and English, and the physical development needed to do the job, as well as classroom-based construction training. They are given assistance such as housing, health referrals, child care, and services related to substance abuse; they work toward their high school equivalency; and there is job-placement assistance over a ninety-day period after graduation.

More than eight hundred residents applied for only seventy-three positions, and budget cuts reduced the class to fifty. Forty completed the program and almost all of those who finished had positive outcomes. Twenty-seven are now employed apprentices in construction trade unions with an average placement wage of $8.50 per hour. This is an impressive result for people who had been labeled as unwilling to work, and therefore not worth investing in.

The mayor also established a business development program. This is a one-year training program in construction skills, life skills, and business and technical assistance to residents of public housing and minority construction contractors. There is also a Youth Entrepreneur Academy. It provides business skills, exposure to real-world opportunities, and knowledge useful in school. One of their projects helps students set up and carry out their own small businesses.

The mayor and his staff focus on investment in people. The division of Family Support Services has established three Family Investment Centers which provide a central point of entry, information, and continuing contact to enable families to avail themselves of a broad range of social programs. Each center has a coordinator who brings together inside and outside services such as day care, Head Start, self-improvement courses, community college opportunities, and the Mayor's Office of Employment Development. Handouts and dependency are not the order of the day. People are helping themselves and helping others to help themselves.

I have heard critics of human services and/or community development argue that such programs stifle individual entrepreneurial activity. Yet human service and community development is often an integral part of very large mainstream economic projects. It appears to be criticized only in projects serving less powerful people.

■ Mechanisms

Lloyd Smith should not have had to risk his own home. For his personal business, yes—but not for a development project that is in the interests of the African-American community, the neighborhood, the city, and the country. Without a better way, such projects won't materialize very often.

There are historical and culture-based structural obstacles here. Black money is mostly new, and investors tend to play it safe. The reluctance of blacks to invest almost kept the MHCDO initiative from getting off the ground. But this is understandable behavior. Businesses looking to invest in the Balkans are seeking government assurances because of the high level or risk. Also, long closed out of entrepreneurial and managerial opportunities, there are too few

Lloyd Smiths. They must be carefully created in large numbers in a short time.

While the 1993 Urban Empowerment Zones and Enterprise Communities legislation will help, such programs generally do not address the limiting effects of past group experiences. Yet the not-so-secret success ingredient in most of the youth and economic projects I have described is the presence of African-American leadership. They build trust, identification, confidence, and show how to effectively manage racial antagonism issues. In these ways they enable families and institutions to help young people develop.

In the last chapter I showed how ethnic group continuity, cohesion, and power created access to mainstream opportunity for their members. Our knowledge of human behavior explains why this is the case. And yet race-specific projects are now illegal or under attack. This makes it difficult to build on the promising practices like the ones described.

And while I have discussed low-income communities, networks of economic, political, and social ties are needed at every level of the black community. Some people support programs that will assist poor blacks but not rich blacks, but economic history shows that networks and connections along the spectrum of wealth are necessary. While such networks can't have the same powerful effect as those that grew out of overall American economic and community development, they can become the foundation for effective community building. Systematic analysis, training, and strategic planning and action can flow from a network- and community-building mechanism.

We must find a way within the spirit and letter of the law to use existing and new community and economic development resources, and still tap into the power of racial pride. Such a mechanism should be based largely on the ideas underlying the youth and economic projects described above. Further elaboration should enable these approaches to promote the level of cohesion and power needed to over-come the effects of past exclusion and continued resistance to black opportunity, participation, and belonging.

My proposal is to create an African-American Foundation and a related Federation. Foundation funds would comple-ment, not replace, other sources of capital for black com-munity and business development. A case could be made here for the government to give additional tax credits for such contributions, which could help stimulate the growth of these funds. One justification for this is that when tax rates were low (one percent until 1945), blacks had little money to contribute, but now that blacks are more prosperous, taxes are high. All Americans should be able to contribute if they wish.

The Federation could be made up of existing organiza-tions with a track record of effective social action, but now geared for a sustained, collaborative, coordinated effort to promote community economic and youth development. The goal would be the preparation of a much larger group of young people who are socialized and able to meet the challenges of a fast-changing mainstream society. Cre-ating training mechanisms to pass on the economic ac-tivity, knowledge, and skills of Lloyd Smith and many others to many young people should be a high priority. A black community Foundation and a Federation are strate-gies for more effective self-help *and* inclusion in the larger society.

As in the projects discussed, a major focus would be on education, the fuel line to the national economic engine as well as community and family functioning. Yet the school is a mainstream institution that too often sends nega-tive messages to minority children, often unintentionally. An African-American community that is organized to pro-tect and promote its children can help them go to school ready to learn, and can complement the work of the school.

The goal must be high expectations for and active promotion of personal excellence among the students, optimal performance among the staff, and fair and responsible support of schools by the society. It is what my parents brought about for me. The community must do the same for all African-American young people today.

CHAPTER
7

SCHOOLS AND THE AMERICAN FUTURE

If we are to successfully create and maintain the three conditions necessary for the survival of our society—a strong economy, communities and families able to carry out their essential tasks, and a cultural belief system that promotes both—schools must play a key role. Democracy cannot work without effective public schools. A science- and technology-based economy has made education more important than ever before.

In 1978, when I was writing my book *School Power*, describing a decade of work in which we had improved the academic and social performance of low-income students, the publisher believed in its importance but doubted that it would sell well because there was no interest in public education. We were entering the high-technology age, and yet most Americans had not come to appreciate the relationship of public education to economic, community, and family functioning.

Five years later, in 1983, Secretary of Education Terrel Bell released the report *A Nation at Risk*, forcing people to pay attention to the problems in public education and the possible negative consequences for our national future. Indeed, that report and others declared that we had a crisis in education. This set off a flurry of activity among most people directly and indirectly connected to public education. At times the tone approached hysteria.

We looked at everything and moved in many directions—reforms in curriculum and instruction, use of technology, effective management of schools, teachers' colleges, and on and on. Some thought too much reform had taken place since the sixties and went back to basics. A very small minority of us looked at learning and development—at the whole child.

In 1989, President George Bush called an education summit. The nation's governors, building on the work of the summit and their own previous initiatives in this area, fashioned six national education goals to be reached by the year 2000. Congress adopted the goals and added two more, passing the 1994 Goals 2000 Educate America Act.

Some feel that we have made significant progress in public education since the education summit in 1989. But many feel that the changes have fallen far short of the need. In his 1995 speech to the National Governors' Association, Louis V. Gerstner Jr., the CEO of IBM, said, "I wonder how many people in our country are committed to achieving those goals. I wonder how many people think we have a *chance* of achieving them. I often wonder how many people even know they exist."

Most of the problem-solving approaches that have emerged to date ignore culture-based structural problems. Nor are they centered on child development. Little attention is being given to the careful selection, preparation, and support of educators. Without addressing these issues and creating coherent policies from the legislature to the classroom, it will be difficult to create an American education system that works well for most students.

Indeed, the message of *A Nation at Risk* and our national response offer a striking example of our usual focus on individual ability and will rather than development. *A Nation at Risk* suggested a single education crisis. But there are at least three major crises—or perhaps three aspects of one.

■ Crisis One

Our students with the highest academic potential are underachieving when compared to their counterparts in nations that are our strongest economic competitors. On the other hand, American students from states with relatively untraumatic social histories have recently done quite well when compared to their counterparts in high-performing nations. A 1995 report shows that eighth-grade students in Iowa, North Dakota, and Minnesota did as well in mathematics as the best performers, Taiwan and South Korea.

In their book *The Manufactured Crisis: Myths, Fraud, and the Attack on America's Public Schools,* David C. Berliner and Bruce J. Biddle point out that critics of U.S. schools have argued that student achievement has declined sharply, while their own review shows that scores on standardized tests of achievement have gone up. Their work is an important counterpoint in an atmosphere of hysteria. But the question still remains whether the improvement is widespread enough to keep up with economic competitors in an age when knowledge is money.

Many young people appear to be unwilling to engage in demanding, rigorous academic work. A highly regarded African-American mathematician told me that he was concerned because he had never had African-American graduate students in his course at a highly selective university. He took a second look and realized that there were no American-born students—black or white—in his class. He was told by his foreign-born students that the American kids said the course was too hard.

The drive for high academic standards is likely to benefit this group most. And the achievement of many in the middle potential group will also likely improve. If not, we will continue to do what we have been doing increasingly: import the work force we need (31.6 percent of recipients of doctorates in 1995 were not U.S. citizens). But the academic-performance focus misses some disturbing trends.

The social pressures on many families are translating to serious student problems. For instance, parents attending a program at a high-achieving, mostly white, affluent suburban school had to walk over drunken students in a stairwell. Another school's administrator, retiring after many years with one of the nation's top schools, told me that he was eager to leave. He complained that he could not keep up with the needs of teens who didn't receive adequate support in families with two parents working, a single parent, or a second marriage.

The 1995 *National Education Goals Report: Building a Nation of Learners* reported that the nation had made no discernible progress toward reducing the percentage of students who admitted to using alchol. The same report also noted that student drug use had increased, as well as the sale of drugs at school.

■ Crisis Two

Most U.S. schools are not providing most young people with the preparation for them to become responsible citizens in an open, democratic society.

"The American Freshman: National Norms for Fall 1995" provides a profile of the attitudes of college freshmen. Let's take a look at what percentage of students considered these objectives to be very important:

Influencing the political structure	17.2 percent
Participating in a community-action program	23.0 percent
Helping to promote racial understanding	33.4 percent
Keeping up to date with political affairs	28.5 percent
Becoming a community leader	29.8 percent

Too many do not participate in the institutions designed to protect democracy. Most students do not know our history, nor can they relate it to our national, or their personal, responsibilities. Many of our students cannot analyze issues and make judgments independent of the rhetoric and demagoguery around them. Too many confuse basic freedoms with frivolous freedoms—self-indulgent do-my-own-thing behavior, which for some leads solely to the accumulation of extreme wealth without paying anything back to society.

For others, the confusion leads to irresponsible conduct, including crime and violence. According to the 1995 *National Education Goals Report: Building a Nation of Learners*, more teachers are reporting that disruptions in their classroom interfere with their teaching. Too many students do not develop the discipline needed to make a commitment to and work toward personal excellence.

Most of these problems have their origin beyond the school, but because schools do not give adequate attention to student development, they cannot address these troublesome tendencies. Schools become victims.

■ Crisis Three

The children of the socially marginal are being denied even minimal learning conditions and, in turn, denying themselves the kind of education they need to succeed in life.

When one student went from the twelfth percentile to the eighty-eighth on a nationally standardized test after a six-week summer course for promising African-American students, I marveled, thinking it was remarkable teaching. She told me it was the first time she had an algebra class. When the state-mandated test had been given previously, she and her classmates were asked to rest their heads on their desk by the school principal.

The 1995 *National Education Goals Report: Building a Nation of Learners* shows that the nation has made no discernible progress toward reducing the gap in college enrollment and college completion rates between white and minority students and toward increasing the number of degrees in mathematics and science awarded to minorities. Also, the gap in preschool participation between rich and poor remains essentially unchanged.

Crises Two and Three are the greatest threat to our national well-being. Crisis Two (citizenship) has been ignored by almost everybody. And Crises Three (reasonable learning conditions) is viewed as such a bedeviling problem that well-intentioned people are ignoring it or looking for quicker and simpler answers.

■ The First Myth and Piecemeal Progress

Our culture's First Myth—that intelligence and motivation alone determine success—impedes our progress. We expect that the bright students will rise naturally to the top. Therefore, we don't have to pay attention to providing children with the developmental experiences that they need. We can also indulge our traditional commitment to local control even when it leads to a harmful, fragmented, ineffective public school system; in this view, schooling is only supposed to give students information.

Schools are being improved in a piecemeal fashion, here and there, through reform efforts across the country. Understandably, though, public and business and political leaders want quick and dramatic progress. And many want inexpensive school improvement or anything that looks and sounds like a solution. Thus a "do something—anything—quick!" mood pervades the country.

One of the latest cure-alls is school uniforms. Helene Grant School in New Haven received national attention when it became one of the first public schools to use student uniforms a decade ago. But the uniform was the least important part of the process. Uniforms grew out of a School Planning and Management Team acting from a comprehensive school plan. An aspect of the plan was to create a climate of participation and belonging. The accepted purpose of such a climate was to promote the development of all students, in the service of academic learning. Yet the idea of uniforms—the quick and easy way—is the only thing that caught on.

This brings to mind another such symbol, the flag.

Recently a principal addressed a conference and described how she had brought about order and improved academic achievement in a previously difficult school. Parents became engaged, and from time to time some were challenged when their behavior was not helpful to their children. The staff provided a focus on what the students could do and not what they couldn't. The adults created a vision of what they wanted for the students and set out to bring it about. In passing, the principal mentioned that one of the rituals they had established to start the day was a flag-raising ceremony.

A light went on for a state legislator in the audience. He said that he thought legislation requiring flag-raising ceremonies in all schools would improve schooling.

Many parents applauded the idea. The principal and staff were more restrained. They knew that his "illumination" reflected several key problems in the efforts to improve schools.

This man was there as a responsible, caring member of the legislature, wanting to do the right thing. As a legislator he was a manager in the third network around the child, the public realm that sets policy. But he had no understanding of the importance of the context—positive beliefs and structures and processes, meaningful interactions among the principal, staff, parents, and students—that helped to make the flag-raising supportive of student development and performance. He did not know why flag-raising ceremonies, by themselves, could not have lasting effects.

The legislator was acting from a control mentality and a belief in the First Myth. "If we can find a way to get the students to behave—patriotism, prayer, meditation, uniforms, whatever—the teachers can teach and the able students can learn." And yet what people who have turned poor schools into goods ones will tell you is that students' success is largely the result of relationships, climate, child development, and *then* learning.

What elements outside and inside their schools made it possible for these two principals—the flag one and the uniform one—to create the climate needed to promote learning and desirable behavior? What had prevented previous principals from doing so with the same community?

I have often heard educators claim that education is complex and difficult to manage because there is no guiding or foundation science. I disagree. The foundation science is *child development.* It should be to education what the basic sciences of anatomy, biology, chemistry, and physiology are to clinical medicine.

In chapter 3 I told of teachers who demanded that the principal remove the social worker who wanted to refer students out for treatment rather than help the students succeed in the school. The teachers were saying, "We need to know more about child development and behavior before we take this job." Schools of education should be called schools of child development and education, which could help establish the importance of and give focus to the discipline of education at the university level.

A child-development focus would suggest appropriate community-family-school policy, preparation and selection of teachers, and the organization, support, and management of schools and school systems. This in turn would affect curriculum and instruction, and promote needed attitudes among all in a school.

Indeed, if we were acting from a child-development perspective, even in hard times we would find a way to better utilize arts and athletics rather than eliminate them. No other curriculum areas put adults in such intimate contact with the young as they engage in stimulating activities that elicit a range of interactions, emotions, thought, and understanding.

Mature adults can help children learn to win, to lose, and to manage either appropriately. And when they fluff a line in the play, or do not handle the win or loss of a game well, they can be helped to get up and try again. It is here that they can learn that a good performance requires hard work and personal discipline. These lessons and skills will be needed in an open, democratic society long after most have forgotten algebra. And if we prepare the adults working with young people well enough, they can help them transfer the joy of good outcomes from disciplined efforts in the arts and athletics directly to reading, writing, math, and science.

■ Centralized Systems

Most of the Western European and Asian countries whose students perform better than ours have more centralized systems. Public education is supported by general tax revenues and assigned to schools on a per-student basis. National standards exist for teacher education and selection, curriculum and instruction, and student performance. Much more time is allotted for staff planning and development, and support for staff and students in these systems is far greater.

In Denmark, the effort called the Folkeskole goes back to the early part of the twentieth century and is the most explicit about the connection between development and learning. So it is helpful to discuss their approach in considering our system. A 1993 Carnegie Corporation of New York report, "Schooling for the Middle Years," describes the essential aspects.

The nineteenth-century philosopher N. F. S. Grundtvig and others wanted schools to address the whole child through a program centered in everyday life and not isolated in academies. Schooling is integrated with community and family life in a way that meets the needs of the developing child. Teachers are expected to get to know each child well through regular contact with families and through the organization and management of the school and classroom work. A stated aim in the 1993 legislative act on Folkeskole reads, "The Folkeskole shall—in cooperation with the parents—further the pupils' acquisition of knowledge, skills, working methods, and ways of expressing themselves and thus contribute to the all-around personal development of the individual pupil."

The approach features a single class teacher for children from seven to sixteen in a caring, protective environment. This is accomplished through small classes, averaging nineteen students, in a small school, with an average size of three hundred children, with a preschool year and an optional tenth year. The class teacher moves with the students from the beginning to the end and has the primary responsibility for student well-being. In some cases a teacher change is made after six years, with the class's second teacher remaining through the ninth year.

The first year, two or three teachers form a team with the class teacher and move up the grade levels with the same students. Together they teach the required subjects. Later on, more subjects are taught and more teachers are involved. But there are no yearly or sudden changes from one to several teachers in different subject areas—nor are there teachers teaching subject matter without planning and sharing with team members. One teacher in each school spends about half his time advising other teachers about how to help students with problems.

The school head, or principal, is selected for training in administration only after having demonstrated excellent teaching and leadership skills. Most continue to do some teaching. Here administration is not a way out of the classroom for people who don't want to teach or are not successful at it. The characteristics that promoted classroom success are raised to the critical leadership level, not the opposite. And a central theme of leadership training is the creation of an environment that makes good development, teaching, and learning possible.

The curriculum includes traditional academic subjects, but compulsory subjects also include Christian studies, art, music, physical education, needlework, metal/woodwork, and home economics. Traffic safety, health, sex education, and family planning must be taught along with experiences that equip students for future educational, vocational, and labor market opportunities. Educational and vocational guidance is compulsory three years before students move into the upper secondary school at seventeen years. Tracking was phased out over a thirty-year period. All schools are now fully comprehensive with a common curriculum until age sixteen.

Although the curriculum is prescribed by the minister of education, decisions about teaching methods and materials are made locally by teachers, principals, parents, and students working collaboratively. In each school five to seven parents elected by other parents serve on a board with two pupils, two teachers, and the principal. The primary task is to promote cooperation between home and school. All of the adults work together to support the development of the students.

A unique and important feature of Danish schooling is a weekly period of free classroom discussion in every grade. Students talk with teachers about the content and method of learning during this period. In this way they share in decision making and responsibility with their teachers. The purpose of the Folkeskole format is to promote personal and social development, individual maturity, and self-reliance. Studies show that young people who share in decision making in warm, supportive environments have fewer behavior problems and are more motivated to achieve at a higher level.

A supportive environment can be created without dampening either the competitive spirit or a personal commitment to the highest level of performance on the part of each student. It is not necessary to create schools and a society with a few winners while giving everyone else a sense that they are losers.

I interviewed a sixteen-year-old Danish exchange student and an hour later interviewed his American classmates in the same school. He spoke warmly of the caring and support he had received in school from the earliest age, about how the teachers treated students like their own children. He told me that this motivated him to do well and to work hard. He explained how teachers kept you "in line" and were available to advise you about all the problems of growing up.

His American classmates said that some teachers care and some don't. They spoke of not having adults to turn to. One complained that the teachers favored the best students. Clearly the experiences of these young people affected their sense of well-being and behavior. Schools are not prepared to respond to this aspect of learning, particularly to young people beyond fourth or fifth grade.

The Danish approach is consistent with the needs of modern society. The last half century is the first time in history that young people have not been raised mostly in close proximity to their parents and the family social network. For the first time, much information comes directly to them from sources other than their parents and other meaningful adults, and they must manage it appropriately in order to develop well.

The Folkeskole provides a sustained presence of parents and other meaningful adults in the lives of young people as they undertake basic tasks—development, learning, and preparation to become responsible adults. It works, in large part, because there is coherence of policy and practice from the legislature to the classroom teacher, developed and maintained through top-down, bottom-up collaboration. It is consistent with Danish cultural values. School staff are prepared to address both student developmental and academic needs.

Parents, students, and the community cooperate and thereby sanction this way of working.

The Danes are generally pleased with their educational system, and they are ranked among the top five nations in the world in economic competitiveness. But they are constantly evaluating the system and looking for ways to make needed adjustments. There is some current concern about reading achievement, but no panic and no quick fixes. No system of schooling is perfect; schooling is an ever-changing process.

I am not suggesting that their model should be copied in America. The size and the racial and ethnic homogeneity of Denmark, and their community and family support programs, have precluded the wide economic gap and cultural network differences that exist in our country. My point is that a focus on child development and the coherent policies that enable teachers and parents to support it are the elements that make good learning, good schools, and a very good school system possible, whether centralized or decentralized.

■ Our Decentralized System

If decentralized systems are to be successful they must provide comparable conditions across the land. There are three major areas in which this could be achieved. The first is providing adequate resources for every district. The second is improving and making teacher preparation comparable for all. The third is preparing school administrators to run their schools better. Let's look at each in turn.

District Funding

Our two 1968 SDP project schools were a microcosm not only of the local system but of our national education system, or systems. Ironically, the latitude of control at the local level has been a major factor in our national education woes. In a decentralized system of schooling, local taxes are used to pay for education. As a result, we do not have an education system. We have at least fifty different education systems. And in reality, each of our fifteen thousand school districts operates autonomously. What we learned from our SDP experiences is that a decentralized school system can work, with child-centered planning and leadership capable of strategic planning at every level. This is less critical in centralized systems serving less diverse student populations.

But in many places local support of schools falls far short, particularly for those most in need. First, local control often does not work as advertised. The common argument holds that people at the local level know and care more about what is in the best interests of their own children. This argument is appealing, but in practice it is irresponsible. The record shows that the most powerful take care of their own and neglect the least powerful.

In the past, local funding of education has led to the deliberate investment of three to seven times (even as much as twenty-five times in some places) as much money in the education of a white child as a black one. Even now a huge disparity exists because many blacks live in areas with low tax bases. A quarter of America's students are in a mere one percent of the school districts, the hundred largest urban districts, which are disproportionately minority. Recent "equity" legislation in Indiana actually decreased funding to cities under economic stress and increased funding to more affluent areas.

Local tax support of education has created great inequities in spending. And as I discussed in chapter 4, the suburban growth that has left those most in need in the cities did not occur wholly by chance. A retired urban teacher who spent his career in schools serving low-income, minority children spent a day in a wealthy suburban elementary school on a bucolic hill. He was treated well by a very competent staff and had a very good experience with sensitive, able students. He said the difference in physical plant, training, and support between his school and this one was "Criminal!"

Every school district is looking for more funds. Block grants to states and other efforts to move decision making closer to where education is offered, without effective safeguards ensuring allocation according to need, is a recipe for greater disaster. The already inequitable distribution of opportunity will certainly be increased and serve to widen the gap between the haves and the have-nots.

Because of the absence of adequate community and family programs, our society, compared to other postindustrial countries, has a disproportionate number of needy families, living under excessive economic and social stress. Too many public schools serving such children receive them underprepared to learn. As a result, too many administrators and teachers, through no fault of their own, are asked to do a job they were not adequately trained to do.

Many parents seek alternatives within the public system when possible, and in private schools when not. Affluent parents use elite private schools even when some would prefer public schools. This reduces the income and race diversity and the opportunity for such groups to gain the kind of understanding and mutual respect that is helpful in a democracy. School leadership must be prepared to successfully bring such groups together. These districts need more financial support, *and* the kind of selection and preparation reforms I will discuss.

While there are excellent and dedicated teachers in low-income areas, for many reasons these districts fare less well in the recruitment competition. Teachers often burn out, and good people often leave, with serious consequences for students, schools, and the society. This most adversely affects students most in need.

Reports in the media about test scores or "newsworthy" incidents of violence, without a discussion of contributing factors, simply make bad matters worse. I was once asked to evaluate an anxious African-American child whose parents had recently moved to a suburban town from the inner city. With a belief based on media reports, her new first-grade teacher expected that she could not read "because inner-city children are far behind." In front of the teacher, the child could not read because she was paralyzed by the teacher's low level of expectations. In fact, the child read well at home and in my office. The price the child paid for the teacher's expectations was confusion and anxiety about her competence.

Teacher Preparation, Selection, and Support

I was a member of the 1996 National Commission on Teaching and America's Future, supported by the Rockefeller Foundation and the Carnegie Corporation of New York. The report says, "Because of a hodgepodge of state and local policies, teachers are unevenly prepared, and well-qualified teachers are unevenly distributed. Standards for teaching vary widely from one state and college to the next." Inadequate teacher-preparation programs are not held accountable. They keep turning out people who are not prepared to teach. And hard-pressed districts keep hiring them.

Some teachers are extraordinarily well educated for their work. But the commission reports:

- In recent years, more than fifty thousand people who lack the training required for their jobs have entered teaching annually on emergency or substandard licenses.
- Nearly one fourth of all secondary teachers do not have even a minor in their main teaching field.
- Among teachers who teach a second subject, 36 percent are unlicensed in the field and 50 percent lack a minor.
- Of high school students taking physical sciences, 56 percent are taught by out-of-field teachers, as are 27 percent of those taking mathematics and 21 percent of

those taking English. The proportions are much higher in high-poverty schools and in lower-track classes.
- In schools with the highest minority enrollments, fewer than half the students get a science or mathematics teacher who holds a license and a degree in the field being taught.

By contrast, ten states ranking at the top by traditional measures have low proportions of unqualified teachers, a greater proportion of smaller schools, and more students taking advanced courses. These are the states with the least traumatic social histories—Idaho, Wyoming, Utah, North Dakota, South Dakota, Nebraska, Kansas, Minnesota, Iowa, and Wisconsin.

And across the socio-economic spectrum, teachers are faced with a new situation. In the past the school was the major source of information, and community conditions made teachers and administrators automatic authority figures with the power to promote desirable behavior. Today students receive much information from other sources—and often more exciting than what they receive in school. Nor is school staff authority any longer automatic. Yet young people are no more mature and disciplined than they were in previous generations. And many will test authority in ways that limit their own development and learning.

Teachers must be prepared to be effective under the new conditions and must be able to do more than just pass on information. They must find ways to create an environment that accords them respect and authority, and to engage students in academic learning. They must enable students to integrate and appropriately use the great amount of information they have, and to take responsibility for their own school learning and behavior.

To do so they must understand how young people develop and learn, and be able to tap into age-related interests that make learning important. For example, young children have an interest in how their bodies work; preteens have an interest in being like adults and teens have an interest in identity issues. Curriculum-based exposure to real-world work and citizenship activities can tap into natural interests in a way that helps young people experience the connection between what they are learning and their future possibilities. Interest in academic learning can be generated among students from all backgrounds when schools can harness inherent interests. Schools can then go with students on a journey of discovery that enables them to think, to integrate and use information to solve problems and manage the world around them, and then move beyond.

To accomplish these tasks, teachers need time to work with each other, with parents, with the community around them, and with individual and small groups of students. They need time to participate in the overall management of the program of their school as well as their own classrooms. In our SDP work, teachers sometimes volunteer their own time to do this, but it is asking too much. American teachers have little or no such time allocated while teachers in other postindustrial countries spend about 40 percent of their time engaged in such activities.

Finally, the powerful impact of teacher attitudes on student performance must be understood by everybody in and related to education. The kind of study and supervision I received in my child psychiatry preparation is expensive and probably can't be duplicated for every teacher. But it was supervision in practice that helped me understand my impact and the impact of each child's experiences, and what to do about it. We are shortchanging teachers by not providing such preparation. I believe that we can better use technology, master teachers, and case studies to help future teachers help students develop and learn. On the other hand, desirable attitudes can't be easily maintained without improving the conditions of teaching.

Too few student teachers are being prepared to work in the new ways. Few districts provide student teachers with the support needed to make the difficult transition from student teaching to teaching. Few provide ongoing coaching and support for teacher development. Few help existing staff adjust to changed needs. And the districts serving the greatest number of families under stress are least able to provide such help.

Leadership

All systems require good leadership. Good outcomes in a decentralized system are even more dependent on good leadership. Each superintendent is a chief executive officer, and each principal is a branch manager. Each must be capable of working with staff to develop a vision, and implement changes, assess them, and adjust them to best serve all staff and students.

Some administrators are well prepared, and some do an excellent job despite the lack of preparation and support. But the system of preparation does not produce the large, consistently excellent leadership pool the nation needs to produce a world-class education system. Excellent principals who mobilize staff and parents and turn their schools around often do so through chance personal attributes and chance school conditions—who and what there is to work with—more than through the processes of preparation and system and community supports. And often, as in the case cited earlier, success is attributed to some peripheral element like a flag-raising ceremony.

Standards for the preparation of administrators vary from state to state, but often a college graduate needs only five courses to become an administrator; at times a master's degree is required. The courses are usually classroom-based, sometimes given by people who have not been in schools for years, often taken at night after work or in the summer. I know of cases in which the five courses were taken over a ten-year period.

Supervised internships are often optional, if available at

all. Also, the supervisor often has no special preparation. A course in human relations may or may not touch on child development. Instruction about strategic management—how to make all aspects of a plan work—is rare. After they get jobs, opportunities for supervisors' professional development and ongoing support range from good to nonexistent. The best administrators are experienced, successful teachers. But by then, with families and other responsibilities, such people cannot afford to return for extended, concentrated management programs.

In Denmark there is no university-based training for administrators. Again, they are selected because they show leadership potential. New school heads are sent to course centers for a week in a group of about twenty-five, where they receive courses in management, economics, law, and child development that are directly related to their school experiences. They return to work but revisit the course center for three days in the same grouping after two to three months. Then they return after a year for another week. This process can be repeated. Meeting together as colleagues from different places and sharing common on-the-job problems and opportunities appears to be very effective. Of course, the cultural context—concern for the common good—contributes greatly to the outcomes.

Michigan recently passed a law that permits untrained administrators! But this appears to be an effort to enable private education companies to import managers who do not have education credentials from the business world—thus discounting education expertise, which needs to be increased among all involved in education, not decreased.

Again, elected officials make important education policies. And most such officials and school board members have no training in administration nor in child development and education. As with the legislator with the flag, these decisions can be made in an unsystematic, uninformed way, and sometimes for dubious troublesome reasons. Too many administrators, teachers, and other school personnel are selected without adequate consideration of competence. And sometimes decisions that should be based on education expertise are instead based on political ideology.

An elected superintendent of education in one Western state came in with the philosophy that the state department should simply send money to local districts and allow them to develop their own programs. The district officials who received the money were unaccustomed to working in this way and didn't use the money well. Whether threatened, defensive, or just in disagreement, state personnel responsible for programs designed to meet particular education needs—for poor children, those with various challenges, and special language needs—attempted to hold on to as much money as they possibly could, and reduced what little communication they had with each other in the first place.

I suspect that some worked for this superintendent's defeat in the next election. He was, in fact, defeated and replaced by one who had his own ideas. Again, the department personnel made adjustments they needed to maintain their programs. This uncertainty, and these survival responses, made cooperation and long-range planning at the state and local levels impossible.

Even efforts to help communities with low tax bases—unless they are coordinated—can create major management challenges. New Haven, Connecticut, is one of the poorest cities of its size in the nation. About seven-eighths of school funding for the year 1995–96 came from outside the local community: $101 million in state aid and $20 million in grants in a total budget of $144 million. The grant money supports *135 different projects*, each with its own priorities, professional development, classroom activities, reporting requirements, and so on.

An enormous amount of administrative coordination is needed. Carlos Mora, a former project director, wrote, "The lack of consistency in action and unity in purpose creates frequent opportunities for conflicts, misunderstandings, and antagonisms." Even well prepared, very good administrators are greatly challenged by the complexity and difficulty of the kind of conditions I have outlined.

■ Current School Improvement Activities

Some of the popular school reform initiatives now being proposed and implemented can be successful—choice (voucher, magnet, and charter are forms of choice) and privatization. There are some very thoughtful, dedicated people supporting these approaches—charter schools in particular. I know parents and school people who are very pleased with the outcomes in certain choice schools.

Nonetheless, these approaches do not address any of the fundamental education problems discussed above. They are simply organizational rearrangements. They improve schools where the necessary combination of people is brought together or exists in the first place, and they often do not include the students most in need.

Our SDP approach, and other child-centered and school-based programs, can't address basic problems—staff selection, preparation, and support. Replication and large-scale school improvement cannot take place through school- and district-based interventions alone. Underperforming schools can't simply learn from or be motivated by successful projects and alternative schools and do better themselves. Our system of education must produce enough teachers and administrators who can create effective child-centered organizations at every school. This can only be done by carefully selecting, preparing, and supporting school staff—which in turn can only be done by making an adequate financial investment in education everywhere.

Some argue that this can be done best by bypassing government bureaucracies and contracting with education entrepreneurs, with the companies and local elected officials held accountable. But bureaucracy is only a part of the problem, and is as much a problem in the private sector as it is in the public. And the profit motive creates other problems. I know of a company that just walked away from one college and signed a contract with its competitor without prior notice. The schools serving the most vulnerable could be hurt the most in such situations.

Anyway, local officials have always been charged with holding public school people accountable. There is little reason to believe that they would be more successful with the private sector. I hear almost no discussion about this among proponents of choice, public or private. Besides, with privatization there is a very good possibility that public money will prepare educators and management for private schools and private profit—and leave the public with the most challenging education problems, the tab for finding a way to address them, and the consequences of not doing so.

Also, using choice approaches would further fragment an already wildly fragmented education system, making it even less likely for a legislature to formulate coherent education policies. And because most schools of choice are using traditional education approaches, they too would leave behind those students most in need.

And remember, students in states and communities with less traumatic social histories are already doing as well on international achievement tests as students in other countries. No form of choice can overcome the complex effects of social trauma on students, families, or education systems. This will require attention to community and family functioning and support for student development.

None of the successful education programs in other postindustrialized nations is moving toward privatization. And what is called private is almost entirely public-supported, and designed to provide learning alternatives to already very effective public systems. With school reform that addresses fundamental problems, the public sector can and should do the job. It is government's responsibility to promote the common good, to pay attention to the needs of all. Public can be good. Our other large public system, the military, is one of the best and most respected organizations in the world.

The military provides our national defense. Public education is a large part of our national offense. We spend almost as much on education as we spend on the military. But we spend almost nothing on education leadership and oversight, and we are haphazard about the preparation and continuing support of education personnel. We can't create a world-class education system while this is so.

■ How We Can Change Our Schools

We can improve our schools most by addressing the problems I have just outlined. School staff must understand child development and learning and how to promote it. The financial support of schooling must be adequate everywhere. The selection, preparation, and support of staff must be based on student needs only. Great attention must be given to providing the best school leadership possible.

What would comprehensive change look like?

We would have a large pool of caring and competent educators and then enhance the conditions that keep them in the field. This would require changing many aspects of the preparation and support of new educators—teachers and administrators—and the retooling and better support of many current practitioners. Also, districts with a low tax base would have to gain the stability that educators and students need to succeed.

Implementing the 1996 recommendations of the National Commission on Teaching and using the 1995 National Council for Accreditation of Teacher Education guidelines for leadership programs would go a long way toward preparing the education workforce we need. These call for administrator preparation that will lead to effective strategic, organizational, instructional, political, and community leadership.

The Commission on Teaching recommendations are keyed to the year 2006:

1. All children must be taught by teachers who have the knowledge, skills, and commitment to teach children well.
2. All teacher-education programs must meet professional standards, or they will be closed.
3. All teachers must have access to high-quality professional development and regular time for collegial work and planning.
4. Both teachers and principals must be hired and retained based on their ability to meet professional standards of practice.
5. Teacher salaries must be based on knowledge and skills.
6. Quality teaching must be the central investment of schools. Most education dollars will be spent on classroom teaching.

To improve teacher education and retraining, I have five proposals that, collectively and in time, could bring about the kind of coherence and quality assurance seen in centralized systems, while maintaining the flexibility of a decentralized system:

1. Professional-development schools
2. An Education Extension Service
3. Leadership academies
4. A Board of Education Masters
5. A human capital–development movement

These proposals would help modify or greatly reduce problematic underlying conditions. The first three would help many education practitioners work differently and more effectively. The final two would help stop the blaming and enable us to begin to address the root causes of our education problems. These are sustainable, supportive, and proactive mechanisms for improving schools—not reactive and punitive.

■ Professional-Development Schools

The National Commission on Teaching strongly endorses professional-development schools. A 1990 report on this new approach, *Tomorrow's Schools,* was issued by the Holmes Group, a consortium of one hundred research universities, after significant study and deliberation. The major goals are to help make educator preparation both more rigorous and more connected to good practice in schools.

In their model the college educator preparatory program is combined with schools in an organic way—much like the medical school–hospital arrangement. This promotes the integration of theory, research, and practice.

Some of the Holmes Group recommendations and those made by the Task Force on Teaching and America's Future are the same. They are (1) that university teachers prepare their students to teach by spending more time with them and with selected supervisory teachers in actual schools; (2) that future teachers learn to teach students how to think and solve problems, and learn how to help students overcome the barriers created by an unequal society; and (3) that future educators be taught in such a way that they themselves become students of learning, and learn to create schools that are learning communities for students.

In short, they call for replacing what amounts to pouring information into the heads of students with engaging them in inquiry and problem solving. This is the kind of workforce preparation that employers are calling for. It is the kind of preparation young people need to be responsible family members, consumers, and citizens.

The recommendations also call for time for classroom teachers to plan, supervise, and reflect with colleagues, as is more often the case in European and Asian schools. And they ask for class scheduling that permits teaching and learning for deep understanding, which is difficult to achieve when the class periods are rigidly scheduled. These changes would promote accountability among students, staff, and parents much more than rules and tests do. Selection, preparation, retention and promotion standards should be based on the ability of teachers and administrators to work in these ways. All of this is needed to promote the kind of staff professionalism that students need.

Coaching or counseling in school-based teacher preparation programs can help future teachers understand that analysis, planning alone and with colleagues, implementation, review of outcomes, and consultation are desirable processes—not a sign of incompetence. Counseling can help some choose another career before they hurt students as well as their own sense of worth. This is done routinely in arts programs in higher education, and it is very much needed in teacher education.

Professional-development schools could help reduce the isolation of the university and the school from the larger world and make learning more meaningful for students and staff. This would lead to the kind of connections between students and the world of work, future family, and citizenship roles that can make education, and the value of personal excellence, more immediate and important to students. Involving organizations and the public in the work of the school would increase knowledge about and support for public education.

Also, improved preparation in general, and development schools in particular, would put educator expertise at the center of the enterprise. I was an early advocate of parent and community participation in support of student development, and I still support such involvement. But I am concerned that in some cases participation has amounted to an adversarial or takeover-of-power mentality. Educators understand that their knowledge must be expanded, that they need to know more about child development and how to promote it. But they still know vastly more than most of us.

Parents can provide wisdom and knowledge about their children and the community. And business and other participants can provide support and access to community resources. And with school staff they can help create a climate that promotes development and desirable performance. But the responsibility for leading the education mission must remain with the educator. And to be effective, educators must promote genuine involvement of these groups.

■ Education Extension Service

This mechanism is needed to help existing practitioners retrain. The model for the Education Extension Service is the Agricultural Extension Service, which was established in the early part of the twentieth century when agriculture was key to the American economy. It was and still is a federal, regional, and state program that provides a range of services to local farmers. The AES has always had access to federal and state funds for the promotion of agriculture. The county agent and associates interact with the local community in ways that inform, support, and "sell" more effective ways of farming. They are often a part of or connected to universities or research institutions where new knowledge is being developed. The work of the Service has helped America to become the breadbasket of the world, and has greatly aided the economy.

Today, improved education is needed to maintain the strength of the American economy. An Education Extension Service could work in a similar way. This could create the coordination needed among federal, state, and district education authorities and other institutions. Indeed, in the past some state departments worked with districts primarily through program support activities. But many have become bogged down in enforcing mandated program regulations, testing, and other administrative operations.

An EES could support teams made up of researchers and successful practitioners in helping other practitioners upgrade themselves. This should include helping local authorities pay greater attention to the careful selection and support of staff—including how to help teachers in need, and how to help them leave with minimal hurt to themselves and others when indicated.

In Denmark teachers work in teams, and new teachers are supported by all the members of their team. They have ongoing discussions and reviews with the school head, also a teacher. With this kind of support and counseling, teachers who are not effective often leave on their own. Counseling of staff who are still not effective after reasonable support efforts is an expected and accepted practice. And much of the help is provided by the local teachers' union. Because of careful selection and strong support, prolonged difficult situations are rare.

Accomplishing these tasks here would require many interactions of all parts of a local community—school personnel, parents, students, and leaders from the full social and economic spectrum. Spontaneous and organized forums and projects are bringing these groups together across the country. An EES could inform these discussions, and sometimes even initiate them.

Informed public discussion would point up intolerable inequities among districts and make denial difficult. This could challenge us to begin to create acceptable learning opportunities and performance standards. Interaction and knowledge sharing would enable local communities to promote and protect public education and to begin to move schools in the right direction.

An EES would be in a position to advise policymakers about the kinds of policies needed. Such a service could help to streamline bureaucracy and spend the considerable amount of money already available in a more efficient and effective way. Indeed, the National Commission estimates that implementing all of its recommendations would cost one percent of what we are paying to bail out the savings and loan associations.

■ Leadership Academies

The impact of efforts to support schooling can be sharply limited by poor leadership. Obviously, the well-prepared leader has the best chance of being effective. Thus, in addition to university leadership degree programs, a postgraduate program for newly appointed and practicing administrators is needed. This academy could be sponsored by the state and/or federal government. In cooperation with extension services and professional-development schools, it could provide knowledge about effective practices and an opportunity to continue to learn and grow with colleagues.

Our Yale School Development Program conducts a one-week Principals' Academy for participating districts each summer. Recent participants commented about how two issues addressed during the week better prepared them for their demanding jobs. The first was the "human factor": how to create conditions that enable the many different people in a school—students, custodians, teachers—to interact well. The second was "pulling it all together": organizing and managing to do all the things a modern school must do—child rearing and development, preparation for testing, drug prevention, and so on. These participants also said the opportunity to get together with peers facing the same challenges in a give-and-take environment was extremely helpful and provided spiritual renewal, learning, and growth.

Because leadership is critical, no superintendent, principal, or school board member should serve without having had an opportunity to learn about both of these factors, and how their performance, good and bad, facilitates or interferes with outcomes for children. For example, case studies of the effects on students of conflicting policies like those of the Western states described in this chapter, could be helpful.

Required attendance in such a program would almost immediately raise the quality of leadership. If all leaders had to participate in training in which they shared and examined their responsibilities in the presence of people from other districts and their own training staff, local authorities would be much more likely to select candidates capable of carrying out child-centered leadership. Leadership academy recognition of localities that greatly improve effective organization building would do more to improve education—and test scores—than rewards for high test scores that are sometimes due largely to the student's family background and social and economic advantages.

Our national defense is so important that the nation built several military academies across the country to find and prepare people for carrying out this mission. The military has multiple ongoing activities akin to leadership academies to provide continued development and readiness. In fact, the armed forces do more training than fighting. The academies are hotbeds and transmitters of the values and ways of the military, and, like principals and school superintendents, military leaders are responsible to elected officials.

In order to produce the highest level of order and effectiveness, the military must operate with a clear chain of command even though, at the highest level, deliberation and appropriate questioning is a part of the process. But clearly leadership preparation for the military is less complicated than for education. To carry out the education mission—teaching and learning—openness, challenge, and deliberation must permeate the entire system. It must take place among the community, district, state, and national authorities.

Before the information explosion there was less questioning. Today, school leaders must be able to maintain their organizations as learning environments and at the same time promote order and the effective growth and development of all involved—in an ethos of questioning.

Education academies need to be structured in line with the mission and needs of education, different from the military's. But they must be given the same kind of attention. While the task is far more difficult, the outcome is no less important.

■ Board of Education Masters

Finally, we need a way to make such changes happen. Deeply rooted in past tradition, the way we educate our children is not going to change unless it can be protected from some of the most harmful influences—extreme funding inequities and poor preparation, selection, and support of educators. At the same time, in a democracy, education legislation must come from elected officials. But again, it should not be constrained by their limited knowledge of the complex enterprise called education, or their political interests.

Existing state and local elected and appointed school boards are largely political entities. We need a way to maintain coherence and continuity of educational practice in the face of the swinging pendulum of political ideologies. Flexibility in the system should be in the interest of meeting educational needs, not political and economic interests.

A useful model here is the way the Board of Governors of the Federal Reserve System serves to promote the economy. We need a Board of Education Masters. The role of this board would be to make certain that education is carried out in a way that is fair for all districts and achieves national and state objectives.

State departments of education often have the incompatible tasks of support to local districts *and* regulatory, performance audit, and sanction activities. These functions need to be separated. State departments of education need to have a collaborative relationship with institutions that can help local school districts, especially university partners and extension services. The audit and sanction functions could become the work of the Board of Education Masters.

As envisioned, the Board would have the power to insist that states and localities meet particular standards. Its members must be highly respected and trusted (even when not liked). Besides possessing a thorough knowledge of education, the Board would have to be selected in a way that protects members from political and economic pressures, even as they are responsible to elected officials. This is how the judicial branch of government was designed. I would suggest that the Board should be under the jurisdiction of the state supreme court, but should be appointed by the court, not elected, through a review process that ensures appropriate expertise and scrutiny by parents and educators.

Such an approach is by no means less democratic than the present process. It actually protects the democratic process. The danger to democracy in the information age, and in turn to children, is the ability of a well-organized few, with a great amount of money and access to technology, to manipulate the facts and promote policies that do not serve the interests of *all* children well.

In order to provide timely information to the Board about all aspects of the conditions and needs of districts, a survey research group, collaborating with state departments of education, could conduct audits to determine whether or not schools are meeting their responsibilities.

Finally, it is impossible to address the education crises fully without changes in financial support of public schools. The great inequities cannot stand. The Supreme Court declined involvement in this matter when it said, essentially, that education was not protected by the constitution in its 1973 ruling on *San Antonio School District v. Rodriguez*. But it is now clear that education is related to the attainment of most other rights protected by the Constitution. As my "no formal education" mother would have said, "That's just common sense!" Inadequate support for education needs to be reconsidered by the Court.

But to be realistic, because our present way of doing things has been so effectively rationalized, the Supreme Court is not likely to act. And not even education masters could change the present financial support arrangement. Indeed, none of the changes necessary to create and support a large pool of educators so that they can effect development and improve levels of learning can happen without a national consensus about what is needed and a call on policymakers to make it happen.

It is for this reason that we need the fifth proposal.

■ Human Capital–Development Movement

The cultural inertia that undergirds the present approaches can only be overcome by a sustained movement that taps deep into our concerns about the kind of future we want for ourselves and all our children. Through a human capital–development movement that rejects scapegoating and insists on problem solving, we would have a chance to make the necessary adjustments to create a world-class education system—which is clearly essential to our goal of the Good Society.

CHAPTER
8

THE GOOD SOCIETY

When I am in southern California I usually walk a couple of miles a day on a track that gives me a sense of the Good Society. It is located in a park that has eight baseball diamonds, two Olympic-size swimming pools, kiddie pools, tennis courts, and game rooms for the less active. Families are often gathered around picnic tables. The last time I was there, a team of young white woman in green-and-yellow sweats were working out on a basketball court. On the adjoining court black teenage males and a few whites were playing a fast-paced game of skins against shirts.

Over the years I've seen men's teams, women's teams, mixed-gender, Hispanic, and mixed-race teams on the baseball diamonds. Once I even watched a hilarious game between fathers and sons under seven, with mothers and fathers cheering every play as though it were the seventh game of the World Series.

The atmosphere there is as friendly and free as anyplace I've been. The day after the 1996 Rose Bowl game, Northwestern against USC, a stranger noticed my Northwestern cap and congratulated me for the showing we made. With one honorary and two earned degrees in my family from Northwestern, I felt ownership although I'm an Indiana grad. That kind of interaction between strangers exists in a park where the cars in the parking lot range from Range Rovers and Cadillacs to Toyotas and Chevys.

The people on the track are of all kinds as well. There are serious joggers and walkers, and there are strollers more interested in conversation and camaraderie than exercise. I have overheard bits of conversations as I pass.

Recently I heard a woman ask, "But what good is it all?" I slowed my pace a bit. She was blond, fiftyish, a professor maybe. She went on to tick off a number of modern scientific and technological miracles and advances—the space shuttle, the Internet, cellular phones, laptop computers.

With each one, her two companions said, "That's progress."

She countered finally, "Is it? More people are out of work, can't take care of their families. And most of us are too selfish to help them."

Now her companions were no longer saying, "That's progress."

She went on, "With the exception of medicine, how has all of this technology business improved the quality of our lives? Most of this stuff just makes life go faster and faster when most of us couldn't keep up in the first place. And a lot of it is no more than fun and games for a few. Who needs five hundred television channels anyway—so what? It doesn't help most people. Look at us. We're in this great park, like paradise, and if we lived five miles away it would be like living in the Third World.

"It's all a big hype. Every new technology company drives the stock market up, and the average age of criminal offenders goes down! And the people in charge don't have the foggiest idea of what to do for the kids—just lock them up, younger and younger. They don't even see the connection between new technology and social pain. Johnson talked about the Great Society. We haven't done much to create it!"

Her companions were now silent, looking down at their sneakers.

She was asking questions I have been asking myself. *Where are we going? Human beings cannot live by science and technology alone. What makes us think we can use science and technology to live the good life individually without creating a reasonable quality of life for everybody, without creating the Good Society? In fact, the knowledge and visibility that technology creates make "not having" much less acceptable than in the past.*

We cannot create a sense of inclusion for all without establishing the Good Society. We cannot create a world-class system of schools without a commitment to the Good Society. As I indicated in the first chapter, the third essential element needed for a society to thrive is a culture that protects both its economy and its families. Such a culture would be the Good Society.

In the 1991 book *The Good Society*, the authors Robert N. Bellah et al., cited the classic criteria—peace, prosperity, freedom, justice. Just as important, they added, "freedom cannot mean simply getting away from other people. Freedom must exist within and be guaranteed by institutions, and must include the right to participate in the economic and political decisions that affect our lives." I would add that behaviors that infringe the rights and opportunities of others are a distortion of freedom that is the by-product of individualism run amok.

Although gains in science and technology are useful, the real challenge to humankind is to create the kind of prosperity, freedom, and justice that will enable us to live together in peace. Events in our own country and around the world—among all racial, ethnic, and religious groups—show that we do not coexist very well.

The Good Society points out that as early as 1915 observers such as Graham Wallas, John Dewey, and Walter Lippmann were stating that changing communication and conditions of commerce would decrease the cohesive power of communities. Dewey in particular recognized that powerful constraints in small communities often limit justice and freedom. He hoped that the institutions being created by changes in technology could both maintain the cohesiveness of communities and promote greater prosperity, freedom, and justice.

Television and the improved speed of travel played major roles in moving us toward the Good Society in the fifties and sixties. The wealth, size, diversity, and creed of America made it a symbol for the betterment of the human condition the world over. Now, for a number of reasons, the opportunity has diminished. Yet we must keep trying.

Human civilization has evolved to contain aggression, a basic instinct both life-sustaining and life-threatening. And people have a powerful impulse to engage with others. The management and healthy expression of these primary impulses has led to the formation of families and schools, museums and galleries, theaters and concerts, parks and gardens, sports and recreation. Our capitalist economic system is probably effective because it permits the outlet of important aspects of aggressive energy—initiative and assertiveness in particular.

On the other hand, our democratic political system is needed to keep the excesses of capitalism in check, and to protect and promote the social structures that favor the expression of positive and caring impulses and relationships. Communities and families do this best. When a society and its culture, and its communities and families, are working well, otherwise murderous human impulses can be modified so that they become individually and collectively gratifying. Thus, a high priority of every society must be to promote desirable community, family, and child development and functioning—the point I have been making throughout this book.

The spirit that grew from the independent, self-sufficient, but mutually supportive farmers in the colonial Massachusetts Bay area led to the America we are proud of and want to sustain and improve. The spirit that grew out of the forced labor of children, Indians, blacks, and whites is the side of our history that embarrasses us and causes the denial that inhibits mature, realistic problem solving.

The denial persists. After a chapter of Christians for Excellence in Education objected, the school board in Hudson, Ohio, would not allow the use of a history book, *The American People,* selected by administrators and teachers for an honors-level course. The major concern was that "too many details on the difficulties experienced by slaves, indentured servants, immigrants, farmers, and industrial workers" were presented in the text.

An important purpose of learning history is to understand the roots of present-day problems and opportunities, not to pass judgment on the mores of a period past. Knowledge of our nation's potential for harmful behavior—as in all human societies—should serve as a reminder of the importance of protecting and promoting the institutions and conditions that reflect our humane side. Accurate knowledge of the past can contribute to sound analysis, better problem solving, and preparation for the future.

■ Effects of Imbalance

The strong aggressive drive in capitalism and the inability of democratic institutions to balance or limit its excesses—greed and selfishness—are factors in the underinvestment in people and the institutions that serve them. They also contribute to the unequal distribution of resources and opportunities within the systems serving people. This has led to wider social and economic ill effects now than in the recent past. A most telling manifestation is the growing deterioration in public conduct, even among those who have had the best opportunities.

A series of examples illustrate this.

On a commuter train from New Haven to New York recently I couldn't help but overhear the conversation of two young black males. One of them looked as though he spent all his time braiding his hair. At a voice level that could be heard by every person in that section of the train, he described his sexual experience with a woman the night before, imitating grunts and groans. Perhaps I'm old-fashioned, but I still think that sexual intimacy should be a private matter, and as an old-fashioned African-American who remains concerned about the plight and image of the community, I found this young man's behavior embarrassing.

A week later on the train I heard almost the same conversation, almost as loudly, from the lips of two young white private school students who sat behind me. The language was a little less colorful—no "motherfuckers," "bitches," and "the nigger said." But it was the same kind of crude, disrespectful, embarrassing discussion.

In the middle of the train, a businessman carried on an angry cellular phone conversation with his office so loudly that it was impossible for anybody in that car to concentrate.

As I left the Lexington Avenue side of Grand Central Station and started up Forty-third Street at midmorning, I encountered a man urinating against a parked truck. This was not a homeless person, or a refugee from a mental health facility. He was a white male dressed in a business suit, with a briefcase at his side. He didn't appear to be a bit concerned about the people around him.

On the train trip home that evening I thought about an experience I had in Stockholm the year before. My colleagues went in a group to a restaurant several blocks away and I had to join them later. I asked the desk clerk whether it was safe to walk alone after dark or whether I should go by cab. She looked at me in confusion. At first I thought she didn't understand English. Then she said, "Oh yes, New York, you're an American. . . . It's safe here, no problem."

When I got to the empty parking garage in New Haven that night, I made my usual cautious scan of the area before moving quickly to my car. But with the events of several weeks in mind I again thought to myself, Where is America headed? And if I had not been a psychiatrist I would swear that a voice came back that said, "I don't know where it's going, but wherever it's going, it's going fast."

I learned from the business news on CNBC television the next morning that the stock market was approaching an all-time high. New technology stocks were leading the way. That afternoon my financial planner informed me that I could afford to live a long time. That should have been good news. But all I could think, given the circumstances, was, Will I find a good place to hide?

Public conduct is only the tip of the iceberg. In spite of the growing number of gated communities, the "haves" are not safe or satisfied. In one such community last year a teenager from a financially privileged background used an automatic weapon to kill his grandparents, his parents, his siblings, and himself. Even with the increased trend of working at home, those who live behind gates are going to have to come and go in a society in which the tone is becoming increasingly angry, mean, punitive, and retaliatory. And most people will not be able to afford to live inside gated communities.

The media and public officials responsible for law and order are giving great play to declining rates of serious crime. But these reports do not forecast tomorrow's story. That story is told in the condition of today's young. The Spring 1996 issue of *Public/Private Ventures News* gave three chilling warning signs:

1. In a few years the United States is going to have the largest number of teenagers it has ever had.
2. While crime has generally declined in many urban and suburban areas, it has spiked sharply over the past few years for teenagers, especially younger ones.
3. The recreational and learning activities and jobs that teenagers need in order to develop soundly are becoming scarcer in the very inner-city and rural areas where much of the bulge in teens will be located. Thus, as youth's numbers rise, there will be—under current conditions and trends—even fewer positive activities to engage them during nonschool hours.

The chapter "The Status of America's Children" in the National Governors' Association report reads:

Available data suggest that each year: 6.5 million children below age six live in single-parent families, 6 million children below age six live in poverty, 3.1 million children below age six are not covered by health insurance. As many as 2 million two-year-olds are not fully immunized against preventable diseases, 1.7 million children between the ages of one and five have elevated blood lead levels, 1.3 million children enter school not ready to learn, and 1.2 million babies are born to unmarried women. More than 1 million children below age eighteen are abused or neglected, more than 1 million children below age five are in inadequate child care settings. Almost 1 million babies are born without the benefit of early prenatal care, 518,000 babies are born to teen mothers, 464,000 children below age eighteen live in foster care, 287,000 babies are born at low birthweight, 222,000 babies are exposed to illegal drugs in utero, 85,000 babies are physically abused, and 33,000 babies die before their first birthday.

What conditions in our society today are going to channel the aggressive energy of these vulnerable young people into constructive pursuits as opposed to crime and other problem behaviors? Our response to date is to continue to blame the most vulnerable for their plight and to turn even more punitive.

■ Pulling Together

Nonetheless, we can still create the Good Society. *A very different cultural mind-set could drive the understanding and behavior of all our institutions, starting from the agreement that life outcomes are not determined by individual intelligence and effort only, but through an interaction between individuals and the policies and practices in the networks around them.*

How do we get there from where we are? We need what I have called a human capital–development movement—involving persons and organizations in family, child development, economic, education, and community areas. People as individuals, busy in their everyday efforts, cannot speak for communities and families as forcefully as powerful groups push economic interests. This creates the imbalance—greater attention to economic matters than community and cultural forces—that hurts all three areas. All three must be in an appropriate and dynamic balance to maintain a vital society.

The elements of a human capital–development movement are already operating, but separately and without sufficient intentionality and power. The values of the Good Society are inherent in the work of family-service- and development-oriented education groups in particular. But all of the health, education, recreation, and other human service people are candidates for participation in an organized, disciplined effort to insist that society give the necessary attention to community and family development and functioning.

The culture of an entire nation is difficult to modify. Some would say it's impossible. And yet, thirty years ago we were a nation of cigarette smokers. Today smoking is largely unacceptable. What got the ball rolling was research, education of cultural leaders, education of the public, and then strong stands by cultural leaders that research evidence and education made possible. The benefit of not smoking began to speak for itself. The high cost of smoking for individuals and the society became more and more apparent. Eventually we had an antismoking movement.

We can move toward the Good Society in a similar way.

The human capital–development movement must drive home the point that exclusion and overblown individualism are harmful to our societal health; it must mobilize communities of people—the powerless and the powerful—committed to the common good. Unfortunately, the harmful effects of excessive individualism and exclusion are not as demonstrable as the harmful effects of cigarettes on physical health.

On the other hand, a huge body of social and behavioral science research shows that good development and a sense of belonging in a supportive environment produce better individual and group behaviors than the opposite. We don't need further sophisticated research. We know better school achievement and better athletic team records are more likely with these conditions. Look at successful school improvement projects. Listen to the players on championship teams tell you why they won. Well-run human organizations strive to promote these conditions—from business corporations to the U.S. military.

A major obstacle is the increasing fragmentation of society. It is more difficult than ever for leaders to influence attitudes and behavior. Leaders have lost much of their power for at least two major reasons. Daily doses of the Vietnam War and Watergate sharply reduced respect for leaders and institutions between 1965 and 1975. And over the past twenty years the inability of leaders to solve pressing problems facing most people have shaken public confidence.

Employment, health care, child care, and other such matters, once managed largely by individuals or their immediate circle, now depend on many factors beyond our direct control and are greatly influenced by people we do not know and will not bump into in church or the local drugstore. A sense of familiarity, predictability, and community is less common.

Just for one example, the same salesclerk at Minas Department Store in Hammond, Indiana, who sold my

mother baby clothing for me also sold us clothing when I
went off to college seventeen years later. Today, such goods
are more likely to be purchased at a chain discount store,
with a different teenager at the checkout counter every six
months.

Identification with the powerful, particularly an employer,
is the way most people experience a sense of belonging and
security, direction and hope. As almost every industry de-
creases its workforce, however, leaders and their institutions
have discouraged worker loyalty. Few leaders are viewed as
effective problem solvers, icons of trust, or bearers of the principles of a good society. Yet our leaders and institutions must
provide the context and basis for decency. All of this has contributed to widespread anxiety and uneasiness.

I recently spoke to a dentist who is retiring after thirty
years of practice in what was once a vital but is now a
declining steel mill town. He told me how his patients once
talked about their churches, their families, their work in the
mill, the political leaders they despised, the ones they loved,
their sadness and joys, and sometimes even their sins. His
concern is that today there is an emptiness and an apathy
even among those who are employed. The only thing most
talk about is the television soaps. "Democracy, freedom, justice, and all that stuff doesn't mean a thing to these people.
They're not involved in anything real." There is despair
about the drugs and crime and violence all around and a
profound sense of helplessness. Most people don't expect
things to get better for their children. Cynicism about religion and politics keeps most from being involved.

This is true not only of working-class areas but also
among professional middle- and upper-class Americans. The
demands of two parents working and the business of living
in complex times—paying for taxes, health care, child care,
and recreation—contribute to an uneasy if not under-siege
mentality. The growing employment uncertainty intensifies
the problem. People who find themselves unemployed and
dependent, having thought this could never be, are devas-

tated. The sense of belonging within a caring society that was taken for granted is slipping away.

■ Unite Around Our Children

Given our sources of paralysis, where is the motivation to create the Good Society to come from? I believe that an effort to provide desirable conditions for our children can create the energy needed for change. What we do for young people—to promote their development and to prepare them for living in a capitalist democratic society—can promote and sustain the Good Society.

In the early days of our school program, there was a city-wide teacher's strike that badly divided our staff. Several efforts to return to the level of civility and collaboration we had worked hard to establish failed. No amount of discussion of the issues worked. Yet when we accidentally began to talk about working together again for the sake of the children, the tide slowly turned.

I was recently asked to cite a couple of key factors that get parents to turn out for school events—high-rise moms on welfare, the working poor, and the tired two-parent working affluent. They all turn out when their own children are on the program. They also turn out when they break bread together with other parents and staff in support of programs *for* their children. I have attended housing-project school programs in which there were huge and enthusiastic parent turnouts.

Parents will sacrifice for their kids, who are our hopes for ourselves, our community, and our society. My parents' hope for a better tomorrow was vested in and enacted in their rearing of me and my siblings. On reflection, this is not surprising. Our desire to nurture our young is what sustains the species.

I was among the throng of Americans who gathered around the Lincoln Memorial in Washington, D.C., on June 1, 1996, to join the Stand for Children. The demonstration, sponsored by the Children's Defense Fund, deepened my conviction that caring about children can be a powerful force for promoting ethical conduct and renewing faith in our institutions. In that crowd of assembled families and more than 3,700 organizations there was an excitement, a sense of hopefulness and determination that is rare in our times.

Most important, young people themselves were involved in Stand for Children, acting constructively on their own behalf and for the common good. This approach has potential not yet fully appreciated. In the follow-up it is likely that ways will be found to regularize such opportunities. There is already evidence that student involvement in peer mediation, gang interaction with adult groups they come to respect, and other activities in which young people can make meaningful contributions can be helpful to them and their communities. But this requires community involvement, which is often absent.

Many in society have been trying to put supportive institutions and programs back in place, but in a piecemeal fashion, without focus, coordination, and empowerment. They have not been put together in ways that allow local people and people from the larger society to interact to support the development of children, neighborhoods, and the society. They often attempt to do for people what people want and need to do for themselves, or do in collaboration with experts. This requires an emotional connection and sense of shared ownership, self-help, and direction.

A different kind of school—a New School—could help put supportive community back together again. Rather than being isolated, it could be fully incorporated into the larger local community and in turn incorporate the larger community into its program. Economic and community development, human services, recreation, and artistic expression programs could be tied to the school setting when possible, or tied to the school, whether on campus or not.

Such a New School could address the two aspects of our

education crisis that are not being given sufficient attention by school-reform efforts. One is preparation of all young people to fully participate in and protect our democratic system. The other is the education of children from families under the greatest economic and social stress. Both crises— but the latter in particular—will require greater integration of the school with community and family service agencies.

Because the purpose of development is to prepare the young to function well as young people and adults, this New School must be geared more directly to what is needed to participate in the economic mainstream. It should directly prepare young people to become successful community and family members and citizens. The New School should be designed—without apology—to help create the Good Society.

In many communities the school is the only mainstream institution still intact, even when it is not functioning well. The social infrastructure needed to enable families to adequately promote the development of the young has been lost. Sometimes there is no source of employment in large areas. Often there are few neighborhood sources of health and child care and other family-support services. Families still intact are often under great economic and social stress. Many communities lack any access to the supermarkets and pharmacies that are ubiquitous in suburbia. Crime and community deterioration go on without hope of stemming the tide. Churches serve the spiritual needs of some, but the feeling of well-being engendered by a caring, nurturing environment cannot thrive in these overall conditions.

There is a growing understanding that many residents of such communities are capable but can't just "do it." In 1989 in Michigan the Muskegon County Community Foundation adopted fifty-four inner-city fifth-grade students, provided a program director, and promised to pay their college tuition. The foundation president, Patricia Johnson, recently indicated that as a result of their intense involvement with this single class of students they now understand the barriers to success. They believe that any significant success will require a team approach from agencies and institutions throughout the community.

The counterargument is: The school is being asked to do too much already, that's why it can't do its real job well. To some extent, I agree. But that is school as we know it. It must change in the ways I described in the last chapter. Once schools are effective organizations, they can move toward greater integration into communities. The New School would need new staff to help engage the community, but not a large number. People in the community organizations they are involved with, including future employers, could become effective helping teachers and helping child developers.

■ The Future Is *Now*

There is movement toward the idea of the New School here and there. In my own experience, soon after John DeStafano was elected mayor of New Haven, we both spoke at a breakfast program sponsored by a service organization. He mentioned to me that he had just been to the funeral of another victim of violence and he wanted that to be the last. He went on to comment with puzzled concern about visiting schools and observing bright, eager, good young children— until about the third grade. And then, he said, something happens to too many that leads to academic decline, violence, and other problems.

My heart leaped. Here was the city's top public official who was not only concerned but understood that there were forces beyond individual ability at play. He also correctly identified the period when the problem becomes apparent. More important, he wanted to do more than lock up youthful offenders and throw away the key. He wanted to prevent the problems. When the opportunity came along, the city made its move.

Led by former secretary Henry Cisneros, the Department of Housing and Urban Development designated fifteen public housing authorities nationwide as Campuses of Learners. Participants were to create "safe and livable communities where families undertake training in new technology and telecommunications and partake in educational opportunities and job training initiatives." New Haven, Connecticut, was designated such a community.

The Housing Authority here is in partnership with the City of New Haven, the New Haven Board of Education, Yale University, Southern Connecticut State University, and the Dixwell and West Rock Neighborhood Corporations, and together they created a Family Campus strategy.

The elementary schools in the two neighborhoods—Wexler School in Dixwell and Brennan School in West Rock—are the cornerstones. A family resource center and multipurpose community center provide an array of support services designed to enable families to carry out their critical tasks, particularly to support the development of their children. The schools are using our COZI model (Comer–Zigler). It joins the early-childhood focus of Dr. Edward Zigler's Schools for the Twenty-first Century concept with our School Development Program, which focuses on creating schools that support the development of children from entry at the elementary level through high school.

The Schools for the Twenty-first Century, initiated by my Yale colleague Dr. Zigler in 1987, is a school-linked child-care and family-support program for children from birth through age twelve and their families. The combined services can enable low-income children to come to school, ready to learn. The components include:

1. All-day year-round child care for children ages three to five
2. Before- and after-school and vacation care for children ages three to twelve

3. Support and guidance in home visitations for parents of children from birth to three years old
4. Information and referral services
5. Support and training to family child-care providers
6. Nutrition and health services

The School Development Program puts the development of the child at the center of the educational process. All of the adult stakeholders—administrators, teachers, support staff, parents, and the young people themselves above elementary school—are involved in developing an environment that nurtures the adults and the students. The School Planning and Management Team of SDP carries out this process and enables the school to coordinate and integrate all of the resources in an orderly fashion, designed to support the development of students.

School and community safety is the number one concern of all parents. Nick Pastore, until recently police chief in New Haven, has been a leading national advocate of community policing. This approach has led to a joint program between the New Haven Police Department and the Yale Child Study Center called the Child Development–Community Policing Program (CD-CP). My colleague Dr. Steve Marans directs the Child Study Center component. Both campuses are a part of the New Haven CD-CP program. The policing teams in the Wexler and Brennan communities are an important component of the Family Campus approach.

In this model, police officers are permanently assigned to neighborhoods and engage in activities that bring them into regular, ongoing contact with children and families within that neighborhood. They are involved in schools and recreational activities, and are sometimes invited to cookouts and a variety of other neighborhood social events. Trust is established, and the police are becoming viewed as helpers more than herders. Community policing is now a citywide effort, and the results have been encouraging. For example, in

1996 a neighborhood management team wrote a letter urging a prosecutor not to plea-bargain with two men suspected of attacking two police officers.

Public housing residents are involved in the management of their complexes and in the design and delivery of health care, child care, housing, policing and other supporting services. They can call on consultants from any of their national and local community partners—university, government, foundations. The idea is to change public housing from a dumping ground of hopelessness and despair that spawns crime and welfare dependency to nurturing environments for living and learning. The underlying assumption is that there can and must be winners and winners rather than winners and losers.

The process is open, collaborative, and involves local citizens in decisions that affect their lives and the lives of their children. And when it isn't, there is discussion and change. This was the approach that mobilized so many parents in the School Development Program. Working together with other residents to achieve their goals creates a sense of shared ownership and connectedness, with each other and with the larger community of work and other service opportunities and responsibilities outside the housing complex.

At the same time, implementing this program has required Yale University president Richard Levin, superintendent of schools Dr. Reggie Mayo, and Mayor DeStefano—some of the most powerful academic and community leaders—to sit in the same room and think together about how to participate in a process that will enable some of the least powerful families to empower themselves and contribute to the mainstream in a positive way.

The plan is for individuals and families to take advantage of programs and resources to build their skills. Some will move from the public to the private housing market. Others who choose to remain in public housing will be equipped to take on new responsibilities and help other families function in a successful way. The education and training, particularly in using modern technology, should prepare the residents for a wide range of employment opportunities. More people with jobs and improved family functioning should increase the rate of school readiness among children in Family Campus neighborhoods.

Connections among community services are expanding. Family Campus staff have been working with the Elm Haven Residents Council, the Elm Terrace Development Corporation, the Housing Authority, the Wexler School faculty and staff, Dixwell church communities, and neighborhood organizations. The Hill Health Center has developed a formal link with Wexler School and has scheduled a pediatrician to consult with the Wexler nurse on a regular basis. They will also provide health education at the school and have arranged for the University of New Haven Dental Hygiene School to conduct dental education and screening.

Varick AME Zion Church has adopted the Wexler School. The parishioners are becoming more involved in the school and working closely with the faculty and staff to maintain a nurturing school environment. Faculty and staff at the Wexler School attended both of our School Development Program one-week training programs to acquire the guiding principles of no-fault, collaboration, and consensus decision making.

The Wexler Family Campus Resource Center recently celebrated the first anniversary of its opening. During that first year the staff provided ongoing parent training workshops, offered GED classes, and operated the Wexler Pride Center, an innovative approach to supporting children who are suspended from class but not sent home (that is, in-house suspension).

A group of African-American males called Men on the Move, led by a male parent of the school, has provided a before-school tutorial program to assist students. This and the Varick Church involvement are like the projects I described in chapter 6. With more systematic organization, school and community resources can be put together to create the seamless web of support children need to develop well and learn.

Brennan Elementary School is in an isolated area of the city with almost none of the services needed to support family functioning. Most of the students are from public housing. It was one of the early School Development Program schools in which social and academic performance improved dramatically. When the test scores began to decline several years ago, I went out to talk to the principal. In less than an hour, five parents stopped by the office to thank her—for rescuing one child from a dangerous family situation and another from a troublesome drug situation, for arranging a hard-to-get health referral, and so on.

What had happened? It turned out that the area had been overwhelmed by a population under even greater economic and social stress than previously. In fact, the principal herself, after visiting the homes of several students, was driving out of the area when someone in a car in back of her was shot. I now could understand the decline in test scores. How could children learn in such an environment? I agreed that the school should do the best it could in instruction, but that it was most important to try to "save the children." The principal needed help outside the school before she could get the test results everybody inside the school wanted.

A school-based clinic has now been placed at Brennan, and arrangements are being made to turn an abandoned building across the street into a family service center. Under discussion is a program that will enable child-care workers to obtain training and to take courses for credit at a local community college. Our COZI program is being implemented to strengthen the academic and social preparation of both students and parents. And the community policing program to help make the area safe is being implemented here as well. Similar projects designed to integrate services so that they better serve family functioning, child development, and school performance are emerging across the country.

When the development of children is a central mission of all services, better ways to integrate and coordinate them become apparent. For example, it is a waste to have a school-based health clinic if the school and health staff don't talk to each other and don't help each other strengthen the curriculum. The school-based clinic staff should be a part of the new faculty, working with teachers, making presentations in science and health in the clinic and the classroom as possible. Curriculum projects with hands-on health providers make their services more acceptable, and they can be additional role models and influential people in the lives of the students.

Interactions with responsible, trusted adults at school, and in a network of activities and services connected to school—the New School—makes school more meaningful. In our SDP Social Skills Program in the mid 1980s we found that preparation for participation in the political and economic arenas gave purpose and direction to learning. Students, parents, and staff came alive. They wanted to know how the world around them works. The classroom teacher—aided by such community leaders as the mayor and the doctor from the hospital—helped them think about how to participate in the world around them. In such settings adults and students alike can begin to raise questions about the appropriateness of the attitudes and values we hold as individuals and as a society.

Today there is much concern about teaching character. But young people can be taught and will best internalize the attitudes, values, and ways we call good character in environments in which they can contribute, feel support, and sense respect and belonging from and with important authority figures.

The project just discussed addresses the third aspect of our education crisis: low-income children and communities that are being denied adequate education, health, housing, and other opportunities, and in turn deny themselves. The New School can also address the second aspect of our education crisis—the failure to adequately prepare most of our young people to participate in a democratic society. The Kids Voting USA project is an important model for doing this among all social and economic groups. It is also an excellent mechanism for bringing all the important networks of a community together to support the development of students at a critical time and in a way that is good for both the students and the society.

The idea for Kids Voting USA began in 1987, when three Arizona businessmen visited Costa Rica and learned that that country had a 90 percent voter turnout, while at that time Arizona ranked forty-second in the nation in voter turnout. Costa Rican observers believed that their turnout had a lot to do with the tradition of young people going to the polls with their parents. This led the Arizonans to develop a pilot program in their state in 1988, which grew into a statewide project by 1990. And that's how a much-needed movement was born.

Barely 50 percent of the voting-age population in our country participate in presidential elections, and only about 30 percent in local elections. Mayors in large and small cities are often elected by a margin of less than 5 percent. Only 42 percent of the people between eighteen and twenty-four years of age are even registered to vote!

In the Kids Voting project, students go to the polls with their parents or adult volunteers (high school students go on their own) and cast their ballots during actual elections. The votes are tabulated and reported in the community media, but of course do not count officially.

Kids Voting is a strictly nonprofit, nonpartisan organization. It is often introduced in a new city by the local business community or by other leadership groups, which then support the schools in carrying out the activity. Often a newspaper publisher takes the lead. Students use newspapers most in their research, and their activities and votes are reported in the papers. Kids Voting personnel train local educators and volunteers with an eye toward helping each child have a good democracy-in-action experience.

While the act of voting has enormous impact on the young people, the process of involving the community and the related curriculum activities have effects that are probably more important and lasting. Knowledge of child development and economic change suggests why this should be.

The habits a society wants adults to hold are established most readily when a child is discovering and establishing "self" in the world beyond family life, particularly between five and twelve. In the agricultural and early industrial age, young children did real work to help the family make it—alongside their parents or other adults. The natural desire to be like and to gain the skills—personal, relationship, and work—of the adults around them was thus automatically satisfied. In contemporary society, the desire is still there, but the opportunity to engage with meaningful adults in activities that help children gain such skills is not. It must be created—and projects like Kids Voting and well-managed arts and athletics programs do provide such opportunities.

The traditional school does not meet this task very well for most students. It provides bits and pieces of information that are unrelated to important problems and are often learned only out of necessity, and by the most disciplined, not always the most creative or otherwise intelligent. A curriculum that addresses real issues, and allows students to use creative ways to obtain knowledge, while interacting with other students and adults who are important to them, can promote interest, self-motivation, and discipline among students who are bored by bits and pieces.

The Kids Voting project, with a curriculum from kindergarten through twelfth grade, is designed to help students feel the power and appreciate the value and importance of voting. And through homework and research using newspapers, the library, the Internet, and other information sources, they also gain the skills of gathering information in different subject areas that will help them make good decisions. They make discoveries for themselves while working in a cooperative setting, and gain firsthand knowledge of the entire election and voting process.

Kindergartners might choose to vote on recess time or snacks and have their names placed on a paper folded as a chain hung under their posted choices so that they can see how their decisions affected the outcome. Middle schoolers could learn that it is important to study the candidates and the issues as when they vote for ice cream (or other enticing choices) without full information, only to discover it is garlic-flavored ice cream. High schoolers can learn how reluctant the most powerful people are to extend the right to vote to all, the pitfalls of majority rule, particularly when there is voter apathy, and the responsibility and benefits of large-scale voter participation in a community.

The students in the Kids Voting program learn how to put themselves in the shoes of others and think about what is right and good for the community. They learn how to discuss the issues with each other, how to tolerate differences of opinion, how to lose and still continue their involvement, how to persuade and work for a cause, and much more. And very important, they often discuss the issues with their parents, providing rare opportunities for parent-child interactions that are not about control of the child's behavior. In fact, the notion of making an independent decision is part of the great appeal to students. The curriculum work makes the act of voting all the more important for everybody.

A teacher in Illinois said, "Kids Voting was so exciting, I'm sad it's over. When can we start again?" A mother in Kansas said, "My daughter was so excited about voting that I decided to vote for the first time and I did." Another said, "I took my twelve-year-old daughter to vote. I also voted, but didn't know how to fill out the ballot. My daughter taught me." A second-grader leaving the polls said, "That was fun! Can I vote again?" A staff member choked up when she described the joy of an immigrant mother who was not yet eligible to vote herself but was able to watch her daughter vote.

The John S. and James L. Knight Foundation has been the principal funder of this program, with several other corporate supporters. In 1996 it was in operation in some schools in forty states and the District of Columbia, involving 4.5 million students, 200,000 teachers, 6,000 schools, 15,000 voter precincts, and more than 75,000 volunteers from every sector of the community. What happens in this project is that all three networks are engaged in supporting the child's overall and citizenship development in a way that is good for the child, good for the program of schools, and good for the society. One teacher participant told me that it is preparation for, participation in, and a celebration of community and democracy all at once!

While experiential preparation for citizenship in a democracy throughout the school years is critical, similar preparation for all the other important aspects of life is just as important. As I mentioned in chapter 3, the parents and students in our SDP project indicated four areas in which students would need preparation to perform adequately as adults: the area Kids Voting addresses, politics and government; business and economics; health and nutrition; spiritual and leisure time. And school is exciting when there is integrated teaching of academic, arts and athletic, social, and emotional skills in these areas.

Many educators agree. But they feel they can't work in this way because keeping their jobs depends more and more on raising test scores. This is ironic and unfortunate: business played an important role in forcing the country to pay more attention to education, but the resultant emphasis on testing is very rapidly and powerfully driving curriculum and instruction in the opposite direction from what is needed to address the concerns of employers. They want people who have a good knowledge base and skills; but, equally important, they want people who can get along and work collaboratively with others, think creatively and solve problems, and work in a disciplined and responsible way.

The traditional bits-and-pieces approach to education produces these outcomes only in that small group of people who can learn in this way because of prior home training or personality. There is a threshold level of whatever it is that intelligence and achievement tests and even school grades measure that is important. But much more is needed to perform well in life.

What is even more frustrating is that cooperative, authentic, or purposeful activity learning like that in Kids Voting and our SDP and other projects produces good test performance in schools where there is stability and continuity of adequate leadership and teaching. It is the kind of teaching and learning that takes place in elite private schools where children achieve well. And because students in communities with less social trauma are achieving as well as top students in other countries, it suggests that the problem is not lazy or inferior educators or students. The problem is our failure to create enough stable, well-functioning systems based on sound child development leading to the ability to handle adult tasks in this more complex time.

Projects that bring community leadership into contact with schools can be helpful in getting at the real problems. The more they observe how hard most educators work, the more they will look beyond the "easy answers" and tendencies to scapegoat school people, students, and their families. The kinds of teaching and learning that are important and how they take place will become apparent, as will the fact that it takes responsible action in all three networks around a child to produce the kind of outcomes we need. We will then have a chance to create the New School across the country.

The New School would in no way be replacing the family. Parent representatives would be involved in management, and parents would be involved in school activities. The New

School is structured to overcome the effects of the break-down in community that has taken place. It is a systematic attempt to knit together the elements of community that once supported families in a natural way. And it is an adjustment to the technology-driven economy and new demands placed on families. It is an effort to complement and support families in their task of preparing their children to become successful workers, family members, and citizens.

The New School can be an important generator of the Good Society. It can create a threshold level of win-win conditions among all—conditions in which most people are able to participate in the economy and meet their needs and responsibilities to themselves, others, and the society.

■ Prevention as the Cure

Several state governors have recognized that addressing the needs of children is a critical way to prevent problems and to promote the kind of society we want. Attention to youth needs at the state level has been growing over the last decade, for young children in particular. All fifty states have taken some action, but generally it has been the states with smaller minority populations, or with unusual leadership, that have moved to community- and family-enabling programs.

In 1994 Vermont governor Howard Dean, M.D., a pediatrician, wrote,

When I became governor in 1991, I was faced with cutting budgets across the board at the same time we were increasing the prison budget by 16 percent. I started asking questions about how to turn things around, about how to decrease the cost of prisons and foster care. The only answer that would address the root of the problem was to start investing early in young children to try to prevent problems from occurring in the first place. . . .

Prevention is everything. Young children who are loved and cared for do not need to be taken out of their home and put in foster care. They are less likely to end up in special education or in programs for severely emotionally disturbed kids. They are less likely to end up in jail when they become teenagers.

It is significant that he is describing the problems and needs of a rural state with racial homogeneity; although Vermont has not had great social turmoil, it has been affected by economic change.

Colorado, led by Governor Roy Romer, and Minnesota, led by Governor Arne H. Carlson, have created new departments of children, youth, and families that will integrate all programs of family functioning and youth development. In Minnesota the state department of education is being replaced by a new department of children, family, and learning. This puts the emphasis on support for development and recognizes its relationship to learning.

Oregon has a State Commission on Community and Family Development, not to study and write reports on poverty but to facilitate family functioning. It has an elaborate plan with measurable benchmarks of achievement. In 1990 West Virginia governor Gaston Caperton created and chaired a cabinet to improve services for families through local family-resource networks. Hawaii—significantly, a state in which the "minority" is the majority—was a pioneer, with Healthy Start in 1985, designed "to enhance parent functioning, encourage optimal child development, and prevent child abuse and neglect."

Ten states have school-linked services, almost twenty have state-level governance structures, ten have family resource centers. But only six have moved to comprehensive efforts that cut across agencies needed to greatly decrease bureaucratic obstacles and to tailor services to developmental needs. The latter is needed in all fifty states before we can send all children to school prepared to learn, can create a world-class system of education, and can prepare all young people for responsible adulthood.

For this to occur in these complex times, much more cooperation and coordination are required among the public, private, and nonprofit sectors than ever before. With good leadership, that sometimes happens. Smart Start, instigated by Governor James Hunt Jr. in North Carolina in 1993, is supported by state tax dollars and private corporate money. The program provides quality day care and health care to thousands of children across the state. But resistance to government involvement is central to our heritage, and has been growing in recent years.

From Habitat for Humanity to numerous school-improvement efforts, many projects have shown the importance of developing programs in a way that enables people to help themselves, and grow and develop in the process. The projects I have cited are evolving from solid, research-based findings. Yet they are fragile new operations being built on political quicksand. It is too easy to confuse the issues, scapegoat less powerful people, and wipe out programs designed to give them a reasonable chance to be constructive participants in the mainstream.

For instance, as an aspect of our School Development Program, in 1995 Edward Murray, a Sacred Heart University professor, developed the SDP Essentials of Literacy Program. Murray piloted the program by entering a school, identifying students who were illiterate, and turning to the students' mothers to assist with the program. The mothers were trained to operate such learning stations as phonics, process writing, and storytelling. The training required was not extensive and the parents were able to help the children in the program in a remarkably short period of time. At the end of sixteen weeks, all the students without exception were literate; nineteen of the twenty-four students showed at least two years of growth, as measured by the state's standardized reading test.

However, a year later the well of parents who were available to assist with the program almost completely dried up. Most of the mothers were on welfare at the time (almost ninety-eight percent of the students at the school were receiving free lunch), and new welfare legislation was passed in Connecticut during that second year that was punitive, intended to "get tough on those deadbeats." The legislation requires the mothers to look for jobs; they don't get them because they can't read well, but they must stand in the employment line anyway. Despite this setback to the pilot program, recently fifteen different cities have contacted Edward Murray and the SDP to replicate the program in their schools.

At juvenile detention centers the reading level of adolescents in advanced groups is about second or third grade; most are at a lower primer level. The correlation between low reading levels, school failure, problem behaviors, and welfare dependency is very strong.

Many Americans have been led to believe that these welfare mothers and fathers and their children are mostly black, and that they are breaking the national bank and are the major cause of national problems. In fact, however, most are white. And recall again, Aid to Families with Dependent Children, Supplemental Security Income, and food stamps—programs for the most dependent—all together amount to only 3.4 percent of the federal budget.

I have been among poor people all my life, and I know that the poor want to work. According to William P. O'Hare (September 1996), "nearly five million adults ages 22–64 worked at least half of 1994, but they earned so little that they and their families were officially poor." A 1996 Rockefeller Foundation report points out that the poor are both rural and urban, and include small business owners, people who work when they can find jobs, and those who have given up looking.

Even responsible political leaders have been put in the ridiculous position of saying they are forcing people—many of whom want nothing more than to be able to work—to get off the dole and go to work. The scapegoat tone, unchallenged, is almost as damaging as the poverty itself. The misinformation is picked up by teacher, employer, and policeman alike, and contributes to negative attitudes and interactions. The public is poorly informed and not in a position to make fair decisions. Vulnerable people already struggling to find a way to experience value and worth are dumped on again.

What happens, though, if more and more people are tossed out of their jobs? There are predictions that the time is right around the corner when very few people will be needed to produce the products of the new age. Even service jobs are being eliminated by technology. Are these people also to become scapegoats?

Our institutions have not been able to adjust fast enough to enable most families to cope with economic changes over the last generation. We will soon need to face the question of how people motivate themselves to develop and perform in a desirable way without work. How will people find meaning and purpose? If "future work" looks more like what we now consider recreation and community service, how will people experience a sense of adequacy and worth as they receive money for what they do? Or is there another way to enable people to purchase necessary goods and services? And if we plan to just allow more and more poverty and alienation, we must be prepared to answer the question put to a "get tough" Pardons Board I served on in 1970 by an already tough warden: "How can I keep this place under control when the prisoners have no hope that good behavior will lead to parole?"

These questions can better be addressed from ongoing, 'o enable communities and families to func-
In chapter 6, I described the kind of effort

that is needed to promote participation and belonging among African-Americans in particular. And while all Americans need to sense inclusion, this can't happen until blacks are no longer in the designated scapegoat role. In the previous chapter I described the need for a school change effort that addresses the foundation and structural issues in education. And in this chapter I have discussed the mechanisms needed to stitch the fabric of community back together in a way that creates a new cultural understanding and tone. There must be an understanding that the individual can function best when all the surrounding networks facilitate the development of genetically determined potentials, and that given the resistance to this notion, a human capital–development movement is needed.

While this movement can't be partisan, such a coalition could develop significant political clout. The operating vehicle might look like the American Association of Retired Persons, with adults as proxies for kids, but kids themselves involved as is possible and age-appropriate. The analytical and propaganda efficiency and effectiveness of the Christian Coalition should be a model.

A significant obstacle is that political advocacy goes against the grain of many in the human services disciplines. At an orthopsychiatry meeting in 1967 I suggested that people in the helping professions needed to influence political practices. A young social worker stood up and screamed at me, "Politics are dirty! I want to help people." In 1996 I spoke to a group made up of the kind of coalition I am suggesting. They were exploring the question of whether they should form a broad-based advocacy association. I look at the tragic conditions of America's children, of many communities and families, and wonder how we can *not* form such a group—not here and there, but at every level nationwide, connected and coordinated. Why did we not do so a long time ago?

Political leaders make the decisions that affect the lives of people, set the tone, and reinforce the beliefs of the country. The New School and the Good Society can't be established without a coalition of mainstream and indigenous community, family, and child service organizations providing informed support to political leaders who recognize the importance of programs that promote people.

EPILOGUE

A little girl's joyous cries of discovery filled the hospital elevator and captured the attention of the several adults riding with her. To the question adults always ask on such occasions, with a proud expression of self she held up the fingers on one hand and said brightly, "I'm five years old!" She followed her parents off the elevator, asking question after question, clearly feeling safe and flourishing in their care.

As we continued to the next floor, the remaining person on the elevator said to me, "How wonderful it would be to experience the world through the eyes of a child again!" I replied, "Hah! I was thinking the same thing."

The encounter caused me to think about both the simplicity and the complexity of life. Life *is* a process of discovery and self-expression that should bring us joy and meaning. But in the human struggle to gain power and control over our own lives, we make it perhaps more difficult than it need be. I thought about how in what now seems like the "golden age" of the 1950s and early 1960s the United States was moving toward creating the conditions that would allow most people to experience a reasonable degree of success and satisfaction. Then I lost the thread of my thoughts in the demands of the day.

A short time later I returned to the town of my birth, East Chicago, Indiana, for the wedding of my niece. While it was a joyous occasion, two things dampened my spirits. When I was a young man there, I had complained that the smoke and soot in the air dirtied my car before I could finish cleaning it. Now the air was clear because the doors of the steel mills were closed, but many people could no longer earn a living to support their families. The second event was the death of Mrs. Smith from a random bullet that struck her as she sat in her own home watching television. No one had yet been arrested, but the suspected cause is a common one in America—teenagers in a street fight.

I know the Smith family well: Mrs. Smith was eighty-two, married to Deacon Smith for sixty-four years. They were hard-working, deeply religious people who had reared six children, two of whom were my schoolmates. Those children are married now with successful grown children of their own. The Smiths are three generations of positive, contributing citizens. They deserved better. We all deserve safety and a chance to experience joy and meaning, particularly after years of responsible and contributing lives. The family was naturally in great pain and furious with the person responsible for Mrs. Smith's death. But they also asked the question we must all answer: "What kind of society creates such monstrous behavior?"

Another former high school mate provided part of the answer. He pointed out that the kids causing serious trouble in the street today would have been working or looking forward to going to work in the local steel mills forty years ago. The casino that stands on the site of a former mill is the major economic replacement, and it is not enough and may not last. And even now, many young people can't meet the social-skill, math, and reading qualifications needed for jobs there. It is interesting that inside the casino, people of different racial groups mix and mingle easily as workers and patrons. Clearly, the core problem today has less to do with race than with the failure to prepare young people for the economy of today and tomorrow. And there must be more varied job opportunities, with more upwardly mobile potential than casinos or steel mills, which require little education anyway and are dead-end jobs.

After discussing these issues and the many challenges of preparing the young with my brother Norman, a recently retired superintendent of schools, I returned home with much apprehension about our national future. But then I remembered that programs to develop communities, families, and schools to bridge the gap *are* working; they simply need to be embraced on a nationwide scale.

Three years ago I lost my wife of thirty-five years, my friend of forty. (I was nineteen and she eighteen when we met.) Her last days at the hospital were excruciating for me. But I had one rewarding experience during that period when I discovered that an intern at the hospital had been a student at our initial project elementary school, Martin Luther King. Her mother had been one of the active parents who returned to school herself, finished college, and became a professional person; her sister became a lawyer and two brothers became engineers. Even in my saddest moments in the hospital, my eyes and ears and heart told me: "These kids can succeed. We *can* have hope."

There are many such stories emerging from many programs across the country. The question is whether America can get rid of the myths, stop the scapegoating, and make the necessary program and policy adjustments to prepare young people from all ethnic and class backgrounds to succeed today and tomorrow. But who will work toward this? Does anybody believe? Does anybody care?

Again, there is cause for hope. I recently received a letter from a very successful businessman and philanthropist who had read an early excerpt from this book in our SDP newsletter, *NewsLine.* He wrote: "I completely agree with you. The notion that human beings are entitled to their successes because of their intelligence and that intelligence is all their own doing, is absurd." His viewpoint is shared by many people across the economic spectrum. And my opinion after fifty years of observation is that there are fewer bad guys than there sometimes appear to be. Most Americans simply want to do the right thing, but in a way that does not jeopardize or ignore their own hopes and needs.

Our mission, if we choose to accept it, is to mobilize the caring majority and insist that our leaders develop policies and programs that enable all our children to have an opportunity to experience joy and constructive self-expression. We must educate policymakers about the faults of the current system and fight for programs that adequately address the needs of America's crumbling social and educational structure.

Schools can't solve our problems, but we can.

NOTES

Chapter 1: My View

A 1996 National Opinion Research Center report:
Cross, Theodore L., Slater, Robert B., and Hoffman, Adonis E. "Vital Signs: Statistics That Measure the State of Racial Inequality." *The Journal of Blacks in Higher Education,* Autumn 1996, 67.

In fact, Aid to Families with Dependent Children:
U.S. Congressional Budget Office. *Appendix J. Budget Tables, Major Spending Categories [by fiscal year, in billions of dollars].* Washington, D.C.: U.S. Government Printing Office, 1995.

The typical child on AFDC:
U.S. Bureau of the Census. *Statistical Abstract of the United States 1995 (115th ed.).* Washington, D.C.: U.S. Government Printing Office, 1995.

But in a recent *New York Times* article:
Prose, Francine. "Outer City Blues: What Began As a Country Utopia for the Parents Turned into a Nightmare for the Kids." *New York Times Magazine,* 21 April 1996, 68.

In his book *Emotional Intelligence*:

Goleman, Daniel. *Emotional Intelligence*. New York: Bantam, 1995.

Sternberg, R. J. "Lies We Live By: Misapplication of Tests in Identifying the Gifted." *Gifted Child Quarterly*, 157–61.

Renzulli, J. S. "Three-Ring Conception of Giftedness: A Developmental Model for Creative Productivity." *South African Journal of Education*, 1985, 1–18.

The proportion of white one-parent families:

U.S. Bureau of the Census. "All Parent/Child Situations, by Type Race and Hispanic Origin of Householder or Reference Person: 1970 to Present." *Current Population Reports, Series P20-483: "Household and Family Characteristics March 1994," and earlier reports.* Washington, D.C.: U.S. Government Printing Office, 1994.

The *Trends* report:

U.S. Department of Health and Human Services, Office of the Assistant Secretary for Planning and Evaluation. *Trends in the Well-Being of America's Children and Youth: 1996.* Washington, D.C.: U.S. Government Printing Office, 1996.

Youth Indicators:

U.S. Department of Education, Office of Educational Research and Improvement. *Youth Indicators 1993: Trends in the Well-Being of American Youth.* Washington, D.C.: U.S. Government Printing Office, 1993.

Because blacks make up only 12 percent of the population:

U.S. Bureau of the Census. *Statistical Abstract of the United States 1995 (115th ed.).* Washington, D.C.: U.S. Government Printing Office, 1995.

The arrest rate for violent crimes for white teens:
Ibid.

Chapter 2: My Window

Wanting to start from the beginning:
Mannix, Daniel P. *Black Cargoes: A History of the Atlantic Slave Trade, 1518–1865*. In collaboration with Malcolm Cowley. New York: Viking, 1962.

In interviewing my mother:
Comer, James P. *Maggie's American Dream: The Life and Times of a Black Family*. New York: New American Library, 1988.

Stanford social psychologist Claude Steele:
Steele, Claude M., and Aronson, J. "Stereotype Vulnerability and African-American Intellectual Performance." In *Readings About the Social Animal*, E. Aronson, ed. New York: W.H. Freeman, 1995, 409–21.

Seven years after I left Howard:
Comer, James P. "The Social Power of the Negro." *Scientific American*, April 1967, 21–27.

Chapter 3: My Work

The foundation sought:
U.S. National Commission on Excellence in Education. *A Nation at Risk: The Imperative for Educational Reform: A Report to the Nation and the Secretary of Education, United States Department of Education*. Washington, D.C.: National Commission on Excellence in Education, 1983.

The work of the SDP was widely known:
Comer, James P. "Educating Poor Minority Children." *Scientific American*, November 1988, 42–48.

In our SDP book:
Smith, Deborah B., and Kaltenbaugh, Louise P. S. "University–School Partnership: Reforming Teacher Preparation." In *Rallying the Whole Village: The Comer Process for Reforming Education,* by James P. Comer, Norris M. Haynes, Edward T. Joyner, and Michael Ben-Avie, eds. New York: Teachers College Press, 1996, 42–71.

In sum, our experience shows:
Haynes, Norris M., Emmons, Christine L., Gebreyesus, Sara, and Ben-Avie, Michael. "The School Development Program Evaluation Process." In *Rallying the Whole Village,* 123–46.

Haynes, Norris M., Gebreyesus, Sara, and Comer, James P. *Selected Case Studies of National Implementation of the School Development Program.* New Haven: Yale Child Study Center, 1993.

Haynes, Norris M., ed. *School Development Program Research Monograph.* New Haven: Yale Child Study Center, 1994.

Cohen, Donald J., and Solnit, Albert J. Foreword to *Rallying the Whole Village.*

Chapter 4: Three Networks and a Baby

Our report, *A Matter of Time*:
Carnegie Council on Adolescent Development. *A Matter of Time: Risk and Opportunity in the Nonschool Hours.* Executive Summary. New York: Carnegie Corporation of New York, 1992.

The report states: "Community organizations provide mentors . . .":
Ibid., page 6.

Hamburg, David A. *Today's Children: Creating a Future for a Generation in Crisis.* New York: Times Books, 1992.

Solnit, Albert J. *When Home Is No Haven: Child Placement Issues*. With Barbara F. Nordhaus and Ruth Lord. New Haven: Yale University Press, 1992.

Chapter 5: Rising Tides and Tied Boats

The largest group of immigrants:
Daniels, Roger. *Coming to America: A History of Immigration and Ethnicity in American Life*. New York: HarperCollins, 1990, 124–25.

The primary wealth of this country:
Comer, James P. *Beyond Black and White*. New York: Quadrangle, 1972.

So pervasive were these forms of servitude:
Pelling, Henry. *American Labor*. Chicago: University of Chicago Press, 1960.

But as a result of the Bacon rebellion:
Higginbotham, A. Leon. *In the Matter of Color: Race and the American Legal Process*. New York: Oxford University Press, 1978.

As Bruce Levine and his colleagues describe it:
Levine, Bruce, Brier, Stephen, Brundage, David, Countryman, Edward, Fennell, Dorothy, and Rediker, Marcus. *Who Built America?: Working People and the Nation's Economy, Politics, Culture, and Society*. 2 vols. New York: Pantheon, 1989, 58.

Between the Revolutionary War and the Civil War:
U.S. Congress. *Congress and the Nation, 1954–1964: A Review of Government and Politics in Post War Years*. Washington, D.C.: Congressional Quarterly Service, 1965, 1027–45.

U.S. Senate Committee on the Judiciary. *Homestead Act Centennial*. 87th Cong., 1st Sess., 1961, 2.

Matthew Josephson:
The Robber Barons: The Great American Capitalists. New York: Harcourt Brace Jovanovich, 1962, 23–24.

The Morgan story:
Chernow, Ron. *The House of Morgan: An American Banking Dynasty and the Rise of Modern Finance.* New York: Atlantic Monthly Press, 1990.

William Zulker describes his rise:
Zulker, William Allen. *John Wanamaker, King of Merchants.* Wayne, Pa.: Eaglecrest, 1993.

James L. Gibbs Jr. and others:
Gibbs, James L., Jr., ed. *Peoples of Africa.* New York: Holt, Rinehart and Winston, 1965.

Mannix and Cowley write:
Mannix, Daniel P. *Black Cargoes,* 119–20.

The many reported cases of "fixed melancholy":
Ibid., 117–20.

Josiah Henson escaped from slavery:
Bayliss, John F. *Black Slave Narratives.* New York: Collier Books, 1970.

In 1837, John C. Calhoun:
"Speech on the Reception of Abolition Petitions," in *Slavery Defended: Views of the Old South,* Eric L. McKitrick, ed. Englewood Cliffs, N.J.: Prentice-Hall, 1963, 13.

The story told by Gerald D. Nash:
A. P. Giannini and the Bank of America. Norman: University of Oklahoma Press, 1992.

In 1785, Congress passed the Survey Ordinance:
Dick, Everett. *The Lure of the Land: A Social History of the Public Lands from the Articles of Confederation to the New Deal.* Lincoln: University of Nebraska Press, 1970.

Jonathan Baldwin Turner:
Deighton, Lee C., ed. *The Encyclopedia of Education.* New York: MacMillan & Free Press, 1971.

Congressman Justin Smith Morrill:
Ibid.

E. Franklin Frazier pointed out:
Black Bourgeoisie. New York: Free Press, 1962.

The proceedings of the National Black Business Association:
Ibid.

The opportunities for industrial jobs:
Lemann, Nicholas. *The Promised Land: The Great Migration and How It Changed America.* New York: Knopf, 1991.

In his book, *Succeeding Against the Odds:*
Johnson, John H., and Bennett, Lerone Jr. *Succeeding Against the Odds.* New York: Warner, 1989.

In a 1920 interview:
Lewis, Ira F. "How C. H. James Rose From a Pack Peddler to Head a Quarter-Million-Dollar Business." *The Competitor,* January 1920.

In *Black Wallstreet*:
Wallace, Ron, and Wilson, Jay J. *Black Wallstreet: A Lost Dream.* Muskogee, Okla.: Black Wallstreet, 1992.

Harry Truman's decision:
Low, W. Augustus, and Clift, Virgil A., eds. *Encyclopedia of Black America.* New York: McGraw-Hill, 1981, 838.

According to Jaynes and Williams:
Jaynes, Gerald D., and Williams, Robin M. Jr., eds. *A Common Destiny: Blacks and American Society.* Washington, D.C.: National Academy Press, 1989, 528.

***Black Enterprise* magazine:**
McCoy, Frank. "Board of Economists Report: A Slower Economy Means Fewer Opportunities for African-Americans." *Black Enterprise,* June 1996.

Wilson, William Julius. *The Truly Disadvantaged: The Inner City, the Underclass, and Public Policy.* Chicago: University of Chicago Press, 1987.

Montgomery, David. *Beyond Equality: Labor and the Radical Republicans, 1862–1872.* With a Bibliographic Afterword. Urbana: University of Illinois Press, 1981.

Chapter 6: Participation and Belonging

Observations made by economists Jessica Gordon Nembhard and Tanya Lewis:
"Biased Tides and Leaky Boats: African-Americans in the U.S. Economy." *An Economic Development Report, Research and Policy Division,* Washington, D.C.: Black Community Crusade for Children/Overview, July 1994. Draft.

John Hope Franklin:
From Slavery to Freedom: A History of African-Americans. With Alfred A. Mass, Jr. New York: McGraw-Hill, 1994.

In *A Hand Up:*
Carson, Emmett D. *A Hand Up: Black Philanthropy and Self-*

Help in America. Washington, D.C.: Joint Center for Political and Economic Studies, 1993.

Resistance in the private sector:
D'Souza, Dinesh. *The End of Racism: Principles for a Multicultural Society*. New York: Free Press, 1995.

And the Carnegie Commission on Science, Technology, and Government:
Science, Technology, and the States in America's Third Century. New York: Carnegie Commission on Science, Technology, and Government, 1992.

In a *Time* magazine article:
Tumulty, Karen. "Why Subsidies Survive: Congress Has Surrendered in the War Against Corporate Welfare." *Time*, 25 March 1996, 46–48.

In a *Harvard Business Review* article:
Porter, Michael E. "The Competitive Advantage of the Inner City." *Harvard Business Review*, May–June 1995, 56.

Yet it should be remembered that "not able" was the argument:
Eddy, Edward Danforth. *Colleges for Our Land and Time: The Land Grant Idea in American Education*. New York: Harper, 1957.

Indeed, even many of those opposed to social investment programs:
Foner, Eric, and Garraty, John A. *Reader's Companion to American History*. Boston: Houghton Mifflin, 1991.

And the black community itself:
Weber, Bruce. "Youthful Pawns with Dreams of Royalty: Chess's Popularity Booms in New York Public Schools with Regular Lessons." *New York Times*, 19 April 1996, B1, B7.

Hugh Price:
"Youth Development: The Overlooked Piece of the Anti-Crime Puzzle." Speech delivered by Hugh B. Price, president of National Urban League at the National Press Club in Washington, D.C., 23 Febrary 1996.

Economist Edward Irons points out:
"The Strength of Enterprise Zones: When Local, State and Federal Governments Collaborate, EZs Can Work." *Black Enterprise,* November 1994, 41.

Current strategies such as Empowerment Zones:
U.S. Department of Housing and Urban Development. *Opportunities for Business in EZ/EC Communities.* Washington, D.C.: President's Community Empowerment Board, 1994.

In Baltimore, under the direction of Mayor Kurt Schmoke:
Housing Authority of Baltimore City. *STEP-UP Program.* 26 October 1995.

While the 1993 Urban Empowerment Zones:
Opportunities for Business in EZ/EC Communities.

One justification for this is that when tax rates were low:
Rubins, Harry. *The IRS—A Little History.* Santa Rosa, Calif.: Rubins Financial Strategies, 1996.

Chapter 7: Schools and the American Future

In 1978, when I was writing:
Comer, James P. *School Power: Implications of An Intervention Project.* New York: Free Press; London: Collier Macmillan, 1980.

Five years later, in 1983:
United States National Commission on Excellence in Educa-

tion. *A Nation at Risk: The Imperative for Educational Reform: A Report to the Nation and the Secretary of Education, United States Department of Education.* Washington, D.C.: National Commission on Excellence in Education, 1983.

In 1989, President George Bush:
U.S. Department of Education. *The U.S. National Education Goals: Strategic Plan for the U.S. Department of Education.* Washington, D.C.: U.S. Government Printing Office, 1994.

In his 1995 speech to the National Governors' Association:
Gerstner, Louis V., Jr. "Education in America." Speech delivered at the National Governors' Association Annual Meeting in Burlington, Vermont, 30 July 1995.

A 1995 report shows that eighth-grade students:
U.S. Department of Education. *The National Education Goals Report: Building a Nation of Learners.* Washington, D.C.: National Education Goals Panel, 1995.

In their book *The Manufactured Crisis:*
Berliner, David C., and Biddle, Bruce J. *The Manufactured Crisis: Myths, Fraud, and the Attack on America's Public Schools.* Reading, Mass.: Addison-Wesley, 1995.

The drive for high academic standards:
"Facts About Higher Education in the U.S., Each of the 50 States, and D.C." *Chronicle of Higher Education,* September 1996.

"Attitudes and Characteristics of Freshman," Fall 1995:
Ibid.

"The American Freshman: National Norms for Fall 1995":
Ibid.

According to the 1995 *National Education Goals Report*:
U.S. Department of Education. *The National Education Goals Report: Building a Nation of Learners.* Washington, D.C.: National Education Goals Panel, 1995.

In Denmark, the effort called the Folkskole:
Carnegie Counsel on Adolescent Development. *Schooling for the Middle Years: Developments in Eight European Countries.* New York: Carnegie Corporation of New York, December 1994.

I was a member of the 1996 National Commission:
National Commission on Teaching and America's Future. *What Matters Most: Teaching for America's Future.* New York: Teachers College, Columbia University, September 1996. Draft.

New Haven, Connecticut, is one of the poorest cities of its size:
Lytle, Tamar. "State Cities Among Worst for Poor Kids." *New Haven Register,* 12 August 1992.

Carlos Mora, a former project director, wrote:
"Progress Report on the Partnership for Minority Student Achievement-New Haven (PMSA)." A Project Funded by the National Science Foundation. New Haven: PMSA, December 1994. Unpublished.

Implementing the 1996 recommendations:
National Policy Board for Educational Administration. *NCATE-Approved Curriculum Guidelines: Advanced Programs in Educational Leadership for Principals, Superintendents, Curriculum Directors, and Supervisors.* NCATE, September 1995.

The Commission on Teaching strongly endorses professional-development schools:
The Holmes Group. *Tomorrow's Schools: Principles for the De-*

sign of Professional Development Schools. East Lansing, Mich.: Holmes Group, 1990.

Spontaneous and organized forums and projects:
"What's To Come Is What Will Count." *New Haven Register,* 10 July 1996.

Darling-Hammond, Linda. "The Right to Learn and the Advancement of Teaching: Research, Policy, and Practice for Democratic Education." *Educational Researcher,* August/September 1996, 5–18.

Schorr, Lisbeth A. and Daniel. *Within Our Reach: Breaking the Cycle of Disadvantage.* New York: Anchor/Doubleday, 1988.

Ravitch, Diane. *National Standards in American Education: A Citizen's Guide.* Washington, D.C.: Brookings, 1995.

Haynes, Monica L. "Studying A Revolution In Education." *Pittsburgh Post-Gazette,* 19 March 1995, A1.

Thompson, Jean, and Daemmrich, JoAnna. "Mayor Orders Changes in EAI Contract." *Baltimore Sun,* 17 March 1995, IA.

Thompson, Jean. "City Scores Rise in All but Writing." *Baltimore Sun,* 21 February 1995, IB.

Chapter 8: The Good Society

In the 1991 book *The Good Society*:
Bellah, Robert N., Madsen, Richard, Sullivan, William M., Swidler, Ann, and Tipton, Steven M. *The Good Society.* New York: Knopf, 1991.

After a chapter of Christians for Excellence in Education objected:
"Minority, Women Coverage Prompts Ohio School Board to Reject History Textbook." *Jet,* 15 July 1996.

The Spring 1996 issue of Public/Private Ventures News:
Walker, Gary. [Untitled article.] *Public/Private Venture News,* 11, 2 (Spring 1996), 1.

The chapter "The Status of America's Children":
McCart, Linda, and Steif, Elizabeth A., eds. "The Status of America's Children." *Governor's Campaign for Children: An Action Agenda for States.* Washington, D.C.: National Governors' Association, 17–21.

In 1994 Vermont governor Howard Dean, M.D., a pediatrician, wrote:
"Success by Six." In ibid., 3.

Hawaii—significantly, a state in which the "minority" is the majority:
In ibid.

According to William P. O'Hare:
"A New Look at Poverty in America." *Population Bulletin,* Washington, D.C.: Population Reference Bureau, Inc., September 1996, 10.

A 1996 Rockefeller Foundation report points out:
The Rockefeller Foundation. *Working It Out: Employment Opportunity as a Route to Self-Sufficiency in Poor Urban Communities.* New York: Equal Opportunity Division of the Rockefeller Foundation, June 1994.

Dryfoos, Joy G. *Full-Service Schools: A Revolution in Health and Social Services for Children, Youth, and Families.* San Francisco: Josey-Bass, 1994.

INDEX

and belief that intelligence
and motivation determine
life outcome, 5, 77, 100
Black access to, vs. other
immigrant groups, 101,
104–5, 119–21
culture and, 86
economic, *see* economic
system
educational, 122–24; *see also*
education
increasing Black access to,
143–48
networks and, 100
origins of, 106–13
political, 119, 120, 121, 128,
130, 138; *see also* political
participation
social, *see* community
Oregon, 227

Pace, Harry Herbert, 127
parents, 42, 193
adolescents and, 92–94
of author, 21–27, 28, 31, 32,
33–34, 86, 87, 98, 99, 126,
130
culture and, 85–86
in first network, 79–87
in School Development
Program, 52–54
see also child rearing; families
Parent Team (PT), 50, 51, 52
participation, *see* belonging and
participation
Pastore, Nick, 216
Peabody, George, 109–10
peer groups, 91–92, 94
Pelling, Henry, 106
Peoples of Africa (Gibbs, ed.),
113
Phelan, James D., 120
political participation:
democratic system and, 10,
203, 204

opportunities for, 119, 120,
121, 128, 130, 138
post-Civil War, 118
schooling and, 169–70
voting project and, 221–24
Porter, Michael E., 144–45
power networks, 108–9, 118
immigrants and, 120
see also opportunity structures
power struggles, 88–89, 93
Price, Hugh, 64–66, 153
Price, Kline, 64
Price, Marilyn, 64
Prince George's County, Md.,
64
private schools, 180, 187, 188
professional-development
schools, 191–93
Project SPIRIT, 151–52
Prose, Francine, 8
public conduct, 204–5, 206
Public Health Service, U.S.
(USPHS), 21, 39, 42
Public/Private Ventures News, 206
punishment and control,
83–85, 88

race, as distraction tactic,
17–18
racial identity, 91, 148
racism, 60, 132
author's experiences of, 17,
18, 20, 29, 33, 34–35
slavery and, 116
Rallying the Whole Village
(Kaltenbaugh and Smith),
68
reading, 80–81
Essentials of Literacy
Program and, 228–29
Reconstruction, 118, 123
Reconstruction Act, 118
recreation, 94–96
Regional Professional
Development Centers, 64